# The Truth-benders

Also by Ronald Seth:

A SPY HAS NO FRIENDS

SPIES AT WORK

A NEW PROSE TRANSLATION OF OVID'S 'ART OF LOVE'

LION WITH BLUE WINGS:
THE STORY OF THE GLIDER PILOT REGIMENT

TWO FLEETS SURPRISED: THE BATTLE OF CAPE MATAPAN

THE UNDAUNTED:
THE STORY OF RESISTANCE IN WESTERN EUROPE

FOR MY NAME'S SAKE: ROMAN CATHOLIC
RESISTANCE TO THE NAZIS AND COMMUNISTS

THE SPECIALS:
THE STORY OF THE SPECIAL CONSTABULARY

THE FIERCEST BATTLE: THE STORY OF CONVOY ONS 5

PETIOT: VICTIM OF CHANCE

STALINGRAD – POINT OF RETURN

OPERATION BARBAROSSA: THE DEFENCE OF MOSCOW

ANATOMY OF SPYING

CAPORETTO – THE SCAPEGOAT BATTLE

FORTY YEARS OF SOVIET SPYING

WITCHES AND THEIR CRAFT

THE FIRST TIME IT HAPPENED

THE RUSSIAN TERRORISTS

THE EXECUTIONERS: THE STORY OF SMERSH

GREAT ENGLISH WITCH TRIALS

THE SLEEPING TRUTH: THE HISS-CHAMBERS AFFAIR

THE SPY IN SILK BREECHES:
THE STORY OF MONTAGU FOX

*Fiction:*

THE PATRIOT

SPY IN THE NUDE

# THE
# TRUTH-BENDERS

*Psychological Warfare*
*in the Second World War*

Ronald Seth

LESLIE FREWIN : LONDON

First published 1969 by
Leslie Frewin Publishers Limited
15 Hay's Mews, Berkeley Square, London W1

Set in Baskerville
Printed by Anchor Press
and bound by William Brendon
both of Tiptree, Essex

09 096120 X

'There is only one way to answer a lie, and that is to tell the truth – even if you have to bend it a little.'

SIR CAMPBELL STUART

# Contents

*Author's Note and Acknowledgements*

1 Words as Weapons 11

2 A Sort of Department 29

3 The White and the Black 43

4 Der Chef 55

5 Rumour 91

6 The Art of Deception 101

7 V for Victory 125

8 For Home Consumption 139

9 Set-piece 149

10 The Inspiration of Private Atack 165

11 The Agony of Naples 175

12 Resistance and Psychological Warfare 183

13 What Justification? 195

*Index* 201

# Author's Note and Acknowledgements

No OFFICIAL HISTORY of the psychological warfare carried out by the British in the Second World War has yet been published. In compiling these stories, therefore, I have had to rely upon the published reminiscences of others, though I have made use of my own researches also.

I have to acknowledge with grateful thanks the permission of the following publishers to quote from, and otherwise draw upon for facts, the books listed below:

Hodder and Stoughton: *Secrets of Crewe House* by Sir Campbell Stuart

Evans Brothers: *The Big Lie* by John Baker White

Cassell and Co: *Their Finest Hour* by W S Churchill

Cassell and Co: *Only the Stars are Neutral* by Quentin Reynolds

Cassell and Co: *The Wounded Don't Cry* by Quentin Reynolds

Cassell and Co: *The Hinge of Fate* by W S Churchill

Secker and Warburg: *The Rise and Fall of the Third Reich* by William Shirer

Secker and Warburg: *Black Boomerang* by Sefton Delmer

Rider and Co: *I Was Monty's Double* by M E Clifton James

Allen and Unwin: *Northcliffe: An Intimate Biography* by H H Fyfe

Evans Brothers: *The Man Who Never Was* by Ewen
    Montagu
Leslie Frewin Publishers Ltd: *The Silent War* by Frank
    Falla

# 1 : Words as Weapons

WHEN THE NAZIS were engaged in their struggle for power, one of the most effective weapons they had in their armoury was propaganda. The ordinary man in the German street had been completely demoralised by the defeat in the First World War. It was all very well for Bethmann-Hollweg, wartime Foreign Minister, on being asked what the Germans would do if they lost the war, seriously to declare, 'We shall organise sympathy'; he did not foresee the economic catastrophe that would overtake Germany as the direct result of defeat; a catastrophe which no amount of sympathy could palliate.

As the post-war economic situation of Germany deteriorated to the point where there seemed no possibility of its eventual recovery, the people were seized by an anaesthetising despair. To stir them at all, Hitler saw that they must have hope restored to them; and the methods which he enjoined on his National-Socialist followers to achieve this aim was an intensive programme of propaganda, in which one of the main slogans was that the only obstacle to Germany's restoration as a great power was the iniquitous Versailles Treaty. Side by side with this was the projection of the Nazi Party as the only party whose ideology fitted the condition of the country in its present state and was capable, therefore, of resuscitating the fortunes of the nation.

How brilliantly this was achieved, the history of Germany between 1933 – the accession of Hitler to power – and 1942 (the turning point of the defeat at Stalingrad) demonstrates. The rallying of practically the whole nation to the banner of the Crooked Cross, within less than a decade, put the erstwhile denizens of the Munich beer-cellar in the corridors of power in the Wilhelmstrasse. Thereafter the dragooning of the nation into an obsequious servant of the Führer's will; the rapid recovery of the economy and industry; the abrogation of the Versailles Treaty with impunity; and finally, the campaign of territorial aggrandisement which led to the Second World War; all transformed Germany from a bankrupt, demoralised country into one that, provided one approved the Nazi way of doing things, allowed a German to lift up his head again, swell with pride and bask in his Führer's reflected glory. No matter how evil one believes the Nazi régime to have been – and it was evil – one must admit that this feat was no mean achievement. The tragedy lay in the refusal of the Nazi leaders to devote their undoubted energies and vision to good rather than evil ends. There are few examples in European history which illustrate so well the axiom that absolute power corrupts absolutely.

The Nazis achieved their absolute power very largely by propaganda. It is one of the great ironies of history that the uses of propaganda were revealed to the Nazis by the fantastic successes achieved by Northcliffe in this field in the First World War.

A successful propagandist in this century requires these qualities above all others: he must be able instinctively to gauge the thoughts and feelings of the masses and by messages that are both simple and attractive he must be able to hold their attention. In addition to being a manipulator of words he must be an organiser. He must think always in terms of numbers – the public, the party – rather than of individuals. He must be active and aggressive rather than objective and matter-of-fact. He must be ethically negative rather than positive; his weapons are exaggeration and false-hood rather than understatement and truth. He must accept as his principal dicta *The greater the lie the less likely will the truth of it be doubted*, and *Constant repetition will eventually achieve acceptance*.

Alfred Harmsworth, Lord Northcliffe, possessed these qualities of the propagandist probably alone among his contemporaries. He had an intuitive grasp of the way in which the masses of Englishmen in the First World War were thinking and feeling; and he realised, possibly also intuitively, though this would be difficult to prove, that to get through to them one had constantly to employ tricks and stunts. Early in the war he saw that morale mattered a great deal and that warfare extended beyond the military sphere. Writing to Asquith, the Prime Minister, in November 1914, he said, 'It is ourselves we have got to defend. . . . I find that whereas there is in Germany immense enthusiasm for the war, there exists in many parts of this country apathy, ignorance or ridiculous optimism, more especially in the provinces.' This, he believed, was not really to be wondered at. Nothing was done to encourage the people who were offered 'nothing but the casualty lists and mutilated scraps with which it is quite impossible to arouse interest or to follow the war intelligently. The public cannot be roused by present methods.'[1]

Long before he was given official approval and the

[1] *Northcliffe: An Intimate Biography:* H H Fyfe: Allen and Unwin, London, 1930.

13

opportunity to put his ideas into practical effect, Northcliffe's propagandist instincts were at work. He lost no opportunity for pointing out to the Government the weakness of British propaganda in Switzerland, the army of anti-Allied propagandists at work in Spain, and such-like facts that had come to his knowledge. In August 1916, he wrote to General Charteris, a member of Haig's Staff, urging that an attempt should be made to 'produce by propaganda a state of mind in the German army favourable to surrender. . . . This bombardment of the mind is almost as important as the bombardment effected by guns'.

Nevertheless, it was not until the beginning of the last year of the war, and then only because of the truly desperate straits in which the Allies were engulfed, that the Government took heed, and appointed Northcliffe to organise and operate what was described as political warfare. Northcliffe acted with his customary energy, and in Crewe House he collected together, under the directorship of Sir Campbell Stuart, a group of writers, journalists and men experienced in politics. The choice is significant, and Hans Thimme in *Weltkrieg ohne Waffen* (published in 1932) appreciates the significance when, though sharply critical of the Crewe House methods, he says that it was distinctly an advantage that none of the men who worked for Northcliffe were 'systemisers or bureaucrats', as the German propagandists tended to be.

The success of Crewe House can only briefly be referred to here. Its principal weapon was the leaflet, dropped over the German lines by balloons or shot over in shells. In August 1918 no fewer than 4,000,000 leaflets were delivered in this way. A trench newspaper in German was specially directed to the soldiers on the Western Front and reached a

14

circulation of half a million copies delivered at regular intervals. One leaflet in particular did much to undermine the morale of the German Navy; it was headed *Germany's 150 Lost U-boats*, and gave details of the fate of 150 U-boat commanders. 'This was a new weapon,' Hindenburg has written in his autobiography, *Out of My Life*, 'or rather a weapon which in the past had never been employed on such a scale or so ruthlessly.' But at the same time that Northcliffe aimed at demoralising the German fighting man, he also tried to give them hope for a better order after the war. Sir Campbell Stuart in *Secrets of Crewe House* says, 'Our aim was to give the German people something to hope for in an early peace and much to fear from the prolongation of the war – that is to make it clear to them that the only way to escape complete ruin would be to break with the system that brought the war upon Europe, and to qualify for admission eventually into the League of Nations on Allied terms'.

After the end of the war, it was widely acknowledged in Germany that Allied and particularly British propaganda had played a definite role in bringing about the collapse of Germany, but as was to be expected, this role came under sharp criticism from the apologists of the collapse. Prominent among these was Dr Edgar Stern-Rubarth, a liberal, a friend of Streseman, once the director of Wolf's Telegraphic Bureau. While admitting to an American audience that the Allies had been fortunate in having in Northcliffe the extremely energetic, capable and unscrupulous organiser that a modern war required, he criticised Northcliffe's methods thus: ' . . . He and his helpers never abstained from utilising even the most untrue and risky arguments for as long as they seemed useful for

15

the purpose'. Differentiating between 'positive' (white) propaganda and 'negative' (black) propaganda, he asserted that the English axiom *Tell a lie and stick to it*, demonstrated a deplorable cynicism, which unfortunately had been the outlook of the British propagandists of Crewe House who had exploited to the *n*th degree the use of 'black' propaganda, i.e. the weaknesses and shortcomings of the other side. So, Stern-Rubarth argued, while 'white' propaganda – the exploitation of one's own strength and accomplishments – could not be criticised, the cynicism and the disregard of positive ethical considerations made illegitimate the use of 'black' propaganda.

The argument about the ethics of Northcliffe's methods continued in Germany for several years after the war, and it is axiomatic that Hitler should have been involved in them. He was full of admiration for British propaganda in the First World War, at the same time that he rejected all German attempts to retaliate. 'What we failed to do', he wrote in *Mein Kampf*, 'was made up for by the enemy with really unheard-of skill and ingenious deliberation.' The Germans, in comparison, had been dilettante and hopeless bunglers. While in England propaganda had been recognised as 'a weapon of the first order', in Germany it had been the occupation of people of little talent, 'the last bread of the politicians without office and a pot-boiler for the modest hero'. One of the great failures of German propaganda, he went on, was the absolutely false impression of the enemy it had created in the mind of the German soldier. While German and Austrian propaganda had poked fun at the enemy, the British had taken the German seriously and depicted him as a barbarian. As a result the German soldier had found a puzzling difference between his foe as depicted by German propaganda, and that same foe's behaviour on the battlefield. Consequently he had lost confidence because of the great discrepancy between the real facts and the wrong image with which he had been presented. In the end he had 'finally dismissed any information he received from his own side as "swindle" and "bunk".'

When *Mein Kampf* first appeared in 1925, the passages on the successes of British propaganda and the failure of the German were ignored, along with the rest of this rather long-winded blue-print for totalitarianism and nationalist action. After 1933, however, what Hitler had written of the German débâcle in 1918 became the official version of German history. The new historians and publicists eagerly spread the view that in the Kaiser's times the German intelligentsia did not understand the real significance and value of propaganda. They attributed the failure of German propaganda in the First World War to this lack of understanding.

It would have been strange indeed that taking Hitler's appreciation of the effect that propaganda can have on people in any given circumstances, if the Nazis had been backward in exploiting it to the full to their own advantage. They were fortunate in having in their ranks a man who, if he cannot be said to have outshone Northcliffe – and this is a debatable point – was in no whit his inferior.

Josef Goebbels, the arch-priest of Nazi propaganda – I would prefer to call him the *deus ex machina* of Hitler's propaganda machine – hero-worshipped Hitler almost from his first personal contact with him. What his beloved Führer thought in the field of propaganda was, like everything else he thought, the equivalent of the synoptic gospels and St John's gospel combined. It was quite fortuitous that Goebbels's talents lay in the propaganda field at the same time that he regarded Hitler as his Christ – and a Christ who saw in propaganda an incomparable weapon for winning the support of the German people.

Goebbels the man is the key to Goebbels the king of propaganda. His youth and immediately subsequent history contain three features which, when recognised, are of considerable importance in understanding the Minister of Propaganda and Public Enlightenment – his deformity (he had a club foot), his low-class origins (one grandfather was a carpenter, the other a blacksmith, his father a clerk in a small gas-mantle factory) and third, his Catholic background.

To compensate for his limp, he sharpened his wit, his congenital restlessness and his malice. 'All his energies,' said Alfred Rosenberg in 1958, 'had to be concentrated on one focal point – to show the others, who were healthy, cheerful and straight, that he, too, could achieve something.' He possessed one physical feature that was strangely at odds with his crippled, small, narrow-chested, excessively hairy body – a beautiful, rich, melodious voice which, combined with his oratorical skill, was one of his main assets as a propagandist.

Josef Goebbels was one of seven children, and the family was involved in a constant struggle to make ends meet. At school, though a good scholar, he was not popular, and since he suffered from the frequent jeers of his schoolfellows at his deformity, he passed a lonely, aloof childhood.

On leaving grammar school in 1917, he decided to study the arts. At this time it was the custom for German students to study at a number of universities. Goebbels indulged this custom to excessive lengths,

18

attending no fewer than eight universities, eventually obtaining his doctorate in philosophy from Heidelberg. He chose to make journalism his career, and tried to join the eminent *Berliner Tageblatt*. His failure to do so accounted for the greater part of his later anti-semitism, for the proprietor and editor-in-chief were both prominent Jews.

In 1925 he became private secretary to Gregor Strasser whom Hitler had put in charge of the Nazi propaganda in the north of Germany. Goebbels applied himself to this work with great enthusiasm and his *amour propre* now received its first fillip from his discovery that he had the gift of speaking in public with great effect. As a consequence of this gift, which he later developed to outstanding proportions, he was in great demand as a speaker at Party meetings.

When he first met Hitler – on 14th February 1926 – Goebbels's initial reaction was one of dislike. However, Hitler, who in his heyday was a shrewd judge of character, recognised the little doctor's potential and set out to win him over. He succeeded completely, and within a few weeks of this meeting, Goebbels was confiding to his diary, 'Adolf Hitler, I love you because you are great and simple at the same time.' Six months later he was appointed Gauleiter of Berlin, and from that moment until his suicide in 1945 (at his Führer's side) he was Hitler's firmest and most loyal supporter.

In the next seven years it was Goebbels who, in his own way, put the Nazis on the political map. Like Northcliffe, he recognised the great potential there was in propaganda and, like Northcliffe, he used every method without a moment's consideration of its ethical rights or wrongs. In November 1928, while still retaining the control of the Berlin Gau, he was appointed by Hitler to be Head of Party Propaganda.

From the moment that he began to survey the disastrous post-war German scene, Hitler was deeply convinced that for any movement that aimed at securing power, propaganda had an essential role. As I have already said, he condemned German propaganda as one of the prime causes of the defeat, and praised British propaganda, which had recognised that the true function of propaganda is to 'convince the masses'. In these views Goebbels wholeheartedly concurred, and it is significant that having appointed him Minister of Propaganda, Hitler informed him that he wished never again to be personally troubled with this most important aspect of controlling Germany; and, indeed, the Führer never once intervened in propaganda affairs.

With their accession to power and the setting-up of the Ministry of Propaganda the Nazis began in earnest their attempt at the wholesale indoctrination of the masses. Goebbels's methods were both complex and simple; complex, because he worked through three agencies – the State Ministry of Propaganda and Public Enlightenment, the central propaganda office of the Party, and the State Chamber of Culture; simple because one man alone visibly controlled all propaganda effort. The Ministry, however, was the hub of the propaganda machine and it was its work that put Goebbels and his achievements on the map.

The main tenet of Goebbels's conception of the nature of propaganda was that to fulfil its aim to form and streamline public opinion, it must be omnipresent. The now famous slogans, *One People, one Nation, one Leader*; *The Jews are our Misfortune*; and *Freedom, Work and Food* were the agents of this omnipresence. They were plastered all over towns and villages, on hoardings along highways; it was impossible to get away from them. But in conjunction with this direct method, more complicated and covert methods were used, that equally, but not blatantly, strengthened the principle of omnipresence. The Press, films, radio, art, literature, the theatre – all were conscripted as propaganda media. Sometimes they were subtle in their approach; sometimes brutally direct; but always striving towards one end – the obliteration of individual opinion and its replacement by Nazi ideology.

All this is not to say, however, that propaganda was used as a mallet, wherewith to bludgeon the people, though the final effect was that this was exactly what happened. Goebbels constantly reminded his officials of the necessity of gauging the moods of the people. Propaganda which did not take the feelings of the people at a particular moment into consideration risked operating in a void, for though outer resistance might be broken down, the breaking down of inner resistance was something very different.

But neither was it enough for the people to be constantly watched. They must also be as constantly occupied in the direction which the State required. The suppression of 'evil' thoughts must be accompanied by the projection of 'approved' thoughts. Though official policies and doctrines were always to be accepted by the propagandists as above criticism, no trick that would make them more palatable should be rejected. Such tricks, too, had to be kept continuously under review, for in time even a trick which had previously been effective could lose its efficacy.

Further, despite the omnipresence of propaganda – which automatically meant that the masses, and not individuals, were exposed to its pressures – Goebbels did appreciate that there existed among the people different levels of intellect, education and interests. Provision had to be made, therefore, for propaganda which appealed to each level. So the artisan was provided with his own specific brand of indoctrination, the peasant his, the intellectual his, the less educated his – though basically the indoctrination was directed towards the same end.

The indoctrination of the German masses, however, was not Goebbels's sole concern. He was also required to project the National-Socialist image abroad, and make it acceptable to people who lived in the comparative freedom of the democracies. His propagandists, therefore, were required to paint the Nazi movement abroad as a respectable, if revolutionary, movement, determined to succeed in restoring Germany's greatness, and a sincere and strong factor in the preservation of the peace of the world. National-Socialism was the great liberator which had overcome the two dragons of unemployment and Bolshevism. 'We believe', Goebbels declared, 'that Europe in the future will be in our debt for our having built a firm wall against anarchy and chaos. Should Germany succumb to Bolshevism, nothing could prevent the entire civilisation of the Western world from being whirled away by its flood.' Germany, he assured all who would listen, was 'ready in all sincerity to co-operate for the peace of the world'.

Though this brief account gives only an outline sketch of the Nazi conception of propaganda, it is sufficient to demonstrate the scientific approach that Goebbels brought to the subject. From 1928 to 1939 he had spent his life organising propaganda campaigns, and studying their effects. By the time that war broke out he had established a machine that had six years' experience on which to draw, and he had a team of highly skilled and intelligent professional propagandists under his control. From 11 a.m. on 3rd September 1939, he was poised to attack.

In order to counteract the devastating potential of the Goebbels lie-factory, an equally powerful weapon was needed on the other side. But despite the fact that Goebbels had based much of his development of words as weapons on the British propaganda methods of the First World War, in 1939 British propaganda was virtually non-existent and Britain's propaganda machine was still in its gestatory stage.

This extraordinary situation had been brought about by the over-zealous patriots who occupied the corridors of power in Whitehall between the wars. This is particularly true of that period in the 1930s during which Goebbels was fashioning his own machine.

Looking back, it seems incredible that after the cataclysmic experience of the First World War there should be any – outside the hard core of reactionary Colonel Blimps – who could imagine that 'things could ever be the same again'. The whole national edifice had been so bombarded by the unnatural stresses and strains of the daily deaths of tens of thousands on the battlefields; by the social revolution which had succeeded from the moment that the first woman had taken her place at the factory bench; by the ethical revolt that had broken out when men escaping briefly from the valley of the shadow of death, tried to obliterate the certain knowledge of their inevitable return to it, submerging themselves in the ecstasy of sexual climax, and when women, appreciating the need of their menfolk for such fleeting oblivion if they were to remain sane, jettisoned the moral rectitude of virginity; by the drain on the national resources in all fields, particularly the financial; that one would have thought that there could never be even an attempt to return to the *status quo ante* of 1914.

There is no doubt that but for the murder of the flower of British manhood on the poppy-strewn fields of Flanders, there would have been a surge forward. As it was, the power of government fell into the hands of elderly men who had served their apprenticeship when the British Empire was at the height of its greatness – for from which ever angle you view it, it *was* a great empire. When they had been young men, there had been no need for the most powerful nation in the world to project her image, for that image had been too substantial to be unknown or disregarded even in the wild Afghan hills, on the plains of Siberia, in the jungles of Africa, in the villages of Turkey and the oases of Arabia. Englishmen, Scotsmen, Irishmen and Welshmen had set a girdle about the world made from their bodies, their thoughts, their ideas, their ideals. The Union Jack flew over the Seven Seas; Britons were almost as omnipresent as their Creator; and this obviated all need for deliberate advertisement. By their deeds, their thoughts and their words they were known.

Somewhat naturally, this inculcated in the Englishman, at any rate, an individual view of his own importance. He had won a great empire, and great empires are not won by men of no character. As with the popular actor who in later life cannot keep up with modern trends and so falls on evil times, so with the British imperial generation memories of the successful past provided a fine avenue of escape from the un-understood things of the present. Unfortunately, memories are phantoms; the present is reality. And it was the imperial generation that occupied the seats of government since there were none younger with experience to do so.

After the political instability of the Twenties, the stability which was so miraculously achieved after the near-extinction of the early Thirties, added to the self-deception of our rulers. It is doubtful whether Stanley Baldwin, John Simon, Samuel Hoare, Neville Chamberlain, Oliver Stanley, Walter Runciman, Lords Hailsham, Swinton, Amulree and Halifax were aware of the changes that had overtaken the nation. Certainly they were completely out of touch with Europe and were blind to the evil already beginning to stalk there. They were still somewhat inclined to despise foreigners because they were not Englishmen, and they despised equally their methods of governing. Foreign relations were little more than the observance of protocol; a knowledge, a real knowledge, of international affairs scarcely existed. Their own form of government they regulated by the rules of cricket, and tried to bring the same rules to bear on those contacts which they had to have with foreign governments from time to time.

It was this regard for 'cricket' and their oversight of the fact that, apart from the Indian Princes, cricket was an exclusively English game not understood by foreigners, which reinforced their basing of the Empire's reputation on its past greatness. There was no greater need in *their* day to advertise Great Britain's superiority than there had been in the hey-day of its might. Indeed, to have blown one's own trumpet would have been degrading and certainly not 'cricket'. Propaganda was, in fact, a dirty word.

That the insidious weapon which Goebbels had forged and was now wielding from the Wilhelmstrasse with ever-increasing effect was a threat to

Great Britain's reputation occurred to few. Even when the urgings of some percipients at last persuaded the Government that it ought to take steps to counter the effects of Berlin's methods of advertising Germany – by charitable bequests abroad and by offering free travelling scholarships to any who liked to apply (to mention only two) – the counter which it permitted itself to use was gentlemanly and too feeble in its impact.

The British Council, inaugurated in July 1935 – two-and-a-half years after the Nazis seized power – had as its objects to make the life and thought of the British peoples more widely known abroad, to encourage the study and use of the English language, to help overseas schools in equipping themselves for this purpose, to enable students from overseas to take courses of education in the United Kingdom, and to publicise British ideals and practices in the realms of science and culture. Today the Council functions all over the world through its British Institutes, its libraries, its courses in English, its exhibitions, films and photographs which portray British life and institutions and in various other ways. In the early pre-war years of its existence, however, its impact was small because distaste for having to do something deliberate about projecting the British image was still such that the funds allotted to it restricted its activities.

The distaste was, in fact a direct result of the inability of the British Government and the majority of the people it represented to accept the fact that the country's image did indeed need boosting. It is possible that this inability was an unconscious reaction to the propaganda of the First World War which had since been revealed as a somewhat sickening business. This assessment was not wholly justified, but the most effective propaganda had been that of accusing the Germans of committing ghastly atrocities, since shown to be false. Northcliffe, unfairly to a large extent, was held responsible for this 'black' propaganda, and had been revealed as a victim of megalomania, the worst form of insanity. His reputation and his methods discredited, there was a feeling that the type of propaganda in which his organisation had indulged was not only un-British but futile.

No thought was given, therefore, to the formation of an organisation which would be able to counteract German propaganda even after war between Britain and the Nazis was seen by many to be inescapable. On the other hand, as it turned out, we were not to be so unprepared propaganda-wise as we were in so many other aspects of fighting a war when hostilities did at last break out.

# 2 : A Sort of Department

It is ironic that one of the chief 'gentlemen' upon whom had fallen the mantle for the control of Britain's affairs, and who believed in conducting those affairs on the basis of the English gentleman's concept of ethical conduct, should have given instructions for starting one of the most effective propaganda machines ever to be operated in the history of the world. A propaganda machine, to boot, which out-Goebbelsed Goebbels in its use of every imaginable lying trick.

When Neville Chamberlain returned from Munich waving the piece of paper which bore his own and Adolf Hitler's signatures to a pledge that 'all future disputes will be settled without force and over the conference table', and spoke of 'bringing back peace with honour', and of 'plucking out of this nettle danger, this flower safety', he sincerely believed that Hitler was as honest a man as he was himself. Like Roosevelt, who became obsessed with the idea that he could 'handle' Stalin and that no one else could, Chamberlain was convinced that by his insistence on bearing himself as an English gentleman in all his contacts with them, he had made such an impression on the German leaders that they, too, in future, would conduct themselves only as English gentlemen.

In their hysterical relief at the breaking of the war-clouds, the British people allowed themselves to be coerced into accepting Chamberlain's assessment of himself as the saviour of the world. They massed in great crowds to mob his motor-car all the way from the airport to Downing Street, and in Downing Street they called upon him, as though he were the Mikado of Japan, to favour them with a glimpse of the glorious radiance of his godlike countenance, and he deigned to grant them their petition.

Now, the British citizens who went out of their minds on that sunny September afternoon in 1938 were not the only people to have greeted the British Prime Minister in this way. As he had driven from his Munich rendezvous with Hitler and Mussolini, the German populace, mostly women and children, had thronged the streets, and cheered him, and showered him with flowers. As he looked at them, ignorant of the fact that Goebbels's machine had ordered them to be there and to cheer, the thought came into his mind that whatever their leaders might have been planning, the good, solid, ordinary German man and woman did not want war. They were as much his allies as the good, solid, ordinary Briton and his wife. If anything were ever to go wrong, and crisis were again to raise its ugly head, they would be on his side; of that he was firmly convinced. He would only have to speak to them, and they would come to his aid. How he would be able to speak to them, he did not at the moment know.

By something of a coincidence, at this time a senior Air Ministry officer was composing a memorandum which he hoped would eventually be read by someone, in the corridors of power, who would be sufficiently impressed by it to give effect to the idea he was putting forward. For some time this officer had been privately worried by a rumour that he knew was current in practically every European country and, so he had heard, throughout the world – that England had no intention of going to war, whatever the Germans might do. Nothing, he said, could be so calculated to whittle away the morale of peoples who still looked upon Britain as the one country which could stand up to Hitler. This was particularly true of the smaller nations: Sweden, Norway, Denmark, Holland and Belgium who, like Czechoslovakia and Poland, were within easy striking distance of Germany's armed might. Traditionally, Britain had always been the protector of the small nation, whether or not formal agreements existed. If these peoples accepted that rumour as true, they would soon be looking for the reason for Britain abandoning her moral responsibilities, and the most likely answer they would get would be that she had not the strength to fight.

One of the most interesting points in the whole situation was the source of the rumour itself. Not a single one of Germany's leaders in any of their public utterances had ever made the faintest allusion to it; and a little probing had made it apparent that the responsibility for its invention and dissemination was Berlin's Ministry of Propaganda and Public Enlightenment. How effective it was could be gauged by the fact that the Hon Joseph Kennedy, American ambassador in London, had been deceived by it, and had informed Washington that on the basis of his own assessment of the situation England would never go to war.

True or false, and whether England had the strength to fight, or whether it was her military weakness that forced the policy upon her, to allow the rumour to go unchecked was tantamount to destroying, by default, any resistance there might be to German plans for securing European and eventual world hegemony. The officer realised that moral strength was not so effective as military might as a deterrent to a would-be tyrant's policies, yet it did have some power of dissuasion. It could win a breathing space of enormous benefit, if ever that should be deemed vital. 'A sort of department,' he suggested, 'should be set up which would let all the world know that the lion had teeth and would use them.'

The officer's immediate superiors liked the memorandum, which was the first document to contain a hint of counter-propaganda, or psychological warfare, and it was passed up the ladder until it eventually reached the Minister for Air, Sir Kingsley Wood. When Wood next met the Prime Minister, he mentioned it, believing that Chamberlain would probably veto the idea out of hand, since it certainly did not conform to the then prevalent notion that counter-propaganda, which, in effect, has no basic dissimilarity from propaganda, was just 'not done' by Englishmen.

As it happened, Wood caught the Prime Minister at a psychological moment. Chamberlain was still deeply concerned with finding ways and means of opening up a direct channel of communication between himself and the German people. It would seem that in his obsessional frame of mind about this, he did not really appreciate the significance of the memorandum's suggestion. Unfortunately, there are no records which could clarify this point, but it is known that he showed great enthusiasm for the project, much to Kingsley Wood's astonishment, and he issued instructions for the setting up of a modest experimental department to consider the possibilities of exploiting some counter-propaganda.

Those who were charged with initiating this instruction for once proved that not all Whitehall is intent on fitting square pegs into round holes. It was recalled that Sir Campbell Stuart, who had worked with Northcliffe in World War I, was still alive; and, what is more, was probably the only Englishman available in England who had had experience of handling propaganda of the type that was needed. When Stuart was approached he was delighted to be of help and swiftly set himself up in a four-roomed office suite in Electra House, off Kingsway, in London. With a staff of three, one typewriter and a slogan, 'There is only one answer to a lie – the truth, even if you have to bend it a little', he was in business.

From early in 1939 it began to become apparent that all the hopes with which Neville Chamberlain had returned from Munich had been false hopes. The culmination of the disillusionment was reached in March. The agreement at Munich, besides giving birth to the scrap of paper on which Chamberlain had placed all his high-minded self-assurance that war had been outlawed, had also given to Hitler, despite Czech protests, certain areas of Czechoslovakia in which lived large numbers of men and women of German origins. The transfer of these areas had scarcely been concluded – people of non-German origin had to be withdrawn and resettled – when Hitler marched his armies into the rest of Czechoslovakia, which was what he had been aiming at all along. The seizure of Czechoslovakia was a repetition of the rape of Austria twelve months before. The Czechs themselves, taken by surprise, made no attempt to resist; all the Western powers could do was to make formal protests.

Even Chamberlain was now left in no doubt that Hitler was not to be trusted, and that despite all his protests about having no desire to go to war with Great Britain, he was not going to permit himself to be deflected from carrying out his programme of German expansion. The Prime Minister at last saw that unless Britain were to isolate herself completely from Europe and abrogate her long-held position of protector of the smaller nations, the time would come when, sooner or later, an armed clash between Britain and the German people 'who wanted peace, whatever their Government might want' would be inescapable.

One other point also became apparent. In *Mein Kampf*, Hitler had set out the programme he intended to carry out to restore Germany to greatness. In the West, and elsewhere, those who read *Mein Kampf* had declared that the programme was merely a blind, contending that no man, however dotty, would reveal to his potential enemies in advance what he intended to do. Now there were some who returned to *Mein Kampf* and were shocked to discover that up to the seizure of Czechoslovakia, Hitler had adhered strictly to his *Mein Kampf* programme. It was incredible! While everyone, Governments included, had been wondering what Hitler would do next, there it had been written down for them to see; to paraphrase Nye Bevan in another context, while they had been gazing into the crystal ball they could have read it all in the book.

Even the British Government seemed to realise this and to accept the principle that if Hitler had stuck to his *Mein Kampf* plan in the past, his success in what he had achieved would encourage him to continue to work by it. The free port of Danzig – taken from Germany by the Versailles Treaty – was next on the list, to be followed by the Polish corridor, which had also been German territory until the formation of the self-determining Republic of Poland as one of President Wilson's Fourteen Points for the reconstitution of Europe after the German defeat in 1918.

To show that the contention that Britain did not intend to fight was a lie, the British concluded a pact with Poland promising to go to her aid if she were ever attacked (France joined Britain in this move). The deeper intention behind the pact was to make Hitler pause and ponder before he did attack Poland – a pause which would give the West the chance to embark on a disorganised flurry in an attempt to make good its military weaknesses. The plan failed for a number of reasons. The lie had actually taken hold of Hitler's ex-commercial-traveller-ambassador in London, Joachim Ribbentrop, and he was now assuring Hitler that even if the British Government wanted to fight, the British people would refuse to, and Hitler had fallen victim to Ribbentrop's assurances. The people, Hitler believed, who would be most likely to cause him trouble were his ideological enemies, the Russians. Even he had not appreciated the savage blow to the efficiency of the Red Army, Navy and Air Force which Stalin's purges had dealt. Stalin, for his part, believed, at this point at all events, that Hitler was bound to attack him sooner or later, and when Hitler made secret advances for not only a non-aggression pact, but a treaty delineating respective spheres of interest which gave half of Poland to Russia, the Russian dictator, as one might have expected, was only too glad to jump at the offer, for, he decided, this would also give him a much needed breathing space in which to build up Russia's military strength. From a more practical angle, Hitler was not impressed by the Western Allies' promise of direct military aid to Poland, for the geographical separation of Poland from the West made the supply of troops

35

and equipment absolutely unfeasible. The only possibility of Western action against Germany was an attack from the West. This Hitler did not fear, because of Ribbentrop's assessment of the British people's will to fight, and also because his intelligence reports gave him a picture of the West's unpreparedness for war; this, though but a partial picture, served to emphasise that the Allies were no serious menace. He saw no reason, therefore, for being deterred from carrying out his programme as planned, notwithstanding any warlike roarings that might come from the West.

While the events of the spring and summer of 1939 were unfolding, Chamberlain seems to have forgotten entirely his former faith in the strength of the simple German's desire for peace, a desire so strong that if he could get through to them they would follow him rather than their Führer. Probably no other British leader, with the possible exception of Stanley Baldwin, has been so ignorant of the character and aspirations of our European neighbours. The mind still boggles at the insularity that could make this possible. However, not only did Chamberlain not remember the great hopes he had had of the German people, he also seems to have forgotten that he had set up a sort of department expressly to provide a link between them and him.

From Electra House came few signs that Sir Campbell Stuart was being very active. True, he had planned and raised Government funds for a film, *The Lion Has Wings*, which aimed at showing that Hermann Goering's Luftwaffe was not the only air force in Europe that had teeth. True, too, it was evident to perceptive listeners-in to the BBC that a guiding propaganda hand was taking a suave and gentlemanly part in broadcasts to Europe.

In fact, Stuart was being more active than appeared. Believing that war was inevitable and imminent, and remembering the success that propaganda leaflet raids over Germany had allegedly had on the morale of the Germans during World War I, he was preparing for similar raids to be made from the very beginning.

Thus it was that people in various parts of England, shortly after nine o'clock in the evening of 3rd September 1939, heard the sounds of aircraft, and remembering the siren that had wailed within minutes of Neville Chamberlain, in the broken tones of a man already broken, announcing that England was at war with Germany, wondered whether they were friend or foe.

After the excitement of the drama that had gone before – the King, controlling with courage the impediment in his speech, had made a firm and resonant manly call to arms which contrasted so vividly with the self-pitiful, yet to-be-pitied, personally disillusioned croak of the Prime Minister – the evening had been subdued. Because of the newly imposed black-out and the unspoken anxiety of wives and children at home, the regulars in the lounge bar of a Lincoln pub, who had hoped by going to the local as usual to prove to themselves as much as to others that Hitler was not going to be allowed to disrupt the habits of a lifetime, self-consciously picked up their torches and the cardboard boxes containing their gas-masks, called good night with a forced bonhomie, and set out for home. As they picked their way carefully through the darkness they heard it!

Growing stronger every minute was the unmistakable sound of heavy aircraft approaching the city. Within minutes, the glasses in the bar they had just left were vibrating on the shelves with a deafening clatter. The two or three most reluctant to admit that war should break the habit of years which had kept them in the bar until mine host called 'Time,' ran down the passage, out through the swing doors and into the High Street. Gazing up at the dove-grey, half-darkened sky they saw them. These were great aircraft, obviously bombers, and since they were climbing still, equally obviously they were British, and were flying east.

Were the rumours wrong, then, that the RAF was under strength in craft and men? On this first night of war, were we carrying death and destruction to Nazi Germany?

Further north in Yorkshire, the people of Driffield were also out in the streets as plane after plane roared over the town, heading east towards the North Sea. Around the airfields in the North and the Midlands that night there was little sleep. Instead there was speculation and unaccustomed feelings of pride mingled with apprehension.

Next morning the BBC's eight o'clock news bulletin put an end to speculation and for many damped their proud hopes. In his crisp impartial BBC voice, Alvar Liddell announced, 'Bomber units of the Royal Air Force carried out a leaflet raid over Western Germany during the night. None of our aircraft is missing'.

Apart from a handful of planners, few realised the significance of this short announcement. It told, in fact, of Britain's first joining battle direct, not with Hermann Goering's Luftwaffe, nor with Keitel's Wehrmacht, nor with Doenitz's navy, but with the Minister of Propaganda and Public Enlightenment, the club-footed, crippled dwarf with the warped mind, Dr Josef Goebbels.

Few people really understood the significance of

38

this first leaflet raid. Few people, in fact, within this island fortress, throughout the whole course of the war, understood the value of the propaganda war being waged on their behalf. This was not their fault, for they did not know about it; and they could not know about it, because had they been told, it might have leaked back to Goebbels and provided him with ammunition to fire back. Even now the part played by psychological warfare, as the propaganda war was officially labelled, is neither fully known nor properly appreciated.

The reaction in Government and Service circles to this first leaflet raid was mixed. Neville Chamberlain recalled his once burning desire to speak direct to the German people, realised that this had at last happened; he was enthusiastic, though he never seemed to grasp the full significance of the raids. Even the more practical Winston Churchill never appreciated that the raids had, in fact, been a tremendous blow to the credibility of the second most important man in the Nazi hierarchy. When Churchill scathingly remarked that he supposed the raids gave the RAF bomber crews good and useful navigational training, he had apparently overlooked Hermann Goering's boast that the RAF would never be able to penetrate the frontiers of Germany. The Germans remembered, however, and though they might have preserved the leaflets for use against the day when toilet tissues in Germany might be hard to come by, they did not forget that the fat, happy Hermann had been given the lie on the very first night of the war.

Though the leaflets prepared by Campbell Stuart might not match the demands of the times, they did at least serve the purpose of highlighting the possibility of providing a counter-blast to the Little Doctor's propaganda war effort. The need for such a counter-blast was to become even more essential within hours of Alvar Liddell's announcement.

Four hours after Neville Chamberlain's declaration of war with Germany, a German U-boat, acting without – even against – instructions had torpedoed the liner *Athenia* off the coast of Ireland. One hundred and twelve people, among them several children and twenty-eight Americans, lost their lives as a result. This jumping of the gun by a U-boat commander momentarily struck panic into the hearts of the German leaders, who feared that the deaths of so many Americans might provoke the United States out of their declared neutrality. It was Josef Goebbels who urged them to be calm; he would set all right.

His efforts to do so produced one of his most remarkable propaganda sallies throughout the whole of the war. By mid-morning of 4th September, the German radio stations were jamming the ether with Goebbels's version of the *Athenia* sinking. The Nazis, he proclaimed, denied, downright and forthright, any responsibility for the liner's end. The man responsible, he declared, was England's amoral monster, the newly appointed First Lord of the Admiralty, Winston Churchill. Churchill, said Goebbels, had caused a bomb to be planted secretly aboard the *Athenia* in order to prejudice Germany's relations with the United States. Though the sophisticated gentlemen in the corridors of power in Oslo and The Hague, in Berne and Budapest, in Belgrade and Athens, in Lisbon and Copenhagen, might smile at the ridiculous nonsense of the claim, many simple, unsophisticated men-in-the-street in all those and many more cities accepted the truth of it. Churchill had a reputation for ruthlessness even then.

As for Sir Campbell Stuart, it is doubtful if he realised quite what he had started with his 'sort of department', despite the doubtful value of his first efforts. Though he was soon to disappear from the scene, his four offices, three assistants and one typewriter were eventually to grow into an Anglo-American operation employing 1500 people in London alone and reaching the peak of its efforts on D-Day, 6th June 1944, when it dropped 27,000,000 leaflets per hour over France.

His modest section was taken over by the Ministry of Information soon after the war began, and then passed under the sway of Dr Hugh Dalton, Minister of Economic Warfare. It was fought over by the British Foreign Office and the Pentagon; generals vied with each other for its services, sometimes coming to the brink of fisticuffs, it is said. Eventually President Roosevelt suggested that it should have its own squadron of aircraft, and his offer to equip it with Flying Fortresses was accepted.

But long before this happened, numbers of Englishmen, not so gentlemanly as Chamberlain and his Government had been in their concept of how the war should be conducted, had taken off their hats and embarked on a war of their own. It was a war in which no holds were barred, and they were soon to prove superior to their ruthless, lying enemy, Josef Goebbels, despite his many years' start on them.

It is interesting to note, however, that propaganda always remained a dirty word in the ears of British politicians. The word itself was never applied to what either the Goodies or the Baddies, the 'Whites' or the 'Blacks', as they were unofficially known, did, either to educate the Germans in the straight truth of what was happening ('white') or to demoralise them with the bent truth – sometimes very bent ('black'). Even when that super-realist Winston Churchill was in supreme command, *propaganda* was never referred to; instead, whatever efforts were made to communicate British ideas to the Germans, whether 'white' or 'black', it was given a much more acceptable – and high-falutin' label – psychological warfare. Nevertheless, though we may smile now at the spinsterish squeamishness of the time, the work that the men who waged both kinds of propaganda war on Germany and the story of their efforts make some of the most interesting and exciting reading that has come out of the Second World War.

# 3 : The White and the Black

As BRITONS STUMBLED and cursed their way through the black-outs of the first wartime winter, one of the additional burdens they had to bear was the BBC broadcasts. From their 'secret' headquarters in Bristol – Goebbels knew where they were going long before they went there – the Variety department filled in the long gaps between more meaty programmes with music played by Sandy MacPherson on an organ in a church hall, alternately with interminable gramophone records.

In London, the Corporation seemed to confine itself to the broadcast of news bulletins, which in those days could contain very little news, since in these months of the Phoney War, as it came to be known, very little was happening anywhere. On Saturdays there were hours and hours of relays of the speeches of politicians from the various public halls where they orated exhortations that often came near to outshining those of the sons of Job. The record in the field was held by the late Oliver Stanley who spoke for three-and-a-half hours. Even Hitler in the full spate of his special brand of hysteria never surpassed this effort.

These exhortations to the British to take heart in the certainty of victory, to fear naught because their destinies were in the best hands, to be patient and tolerant of all difficulties of rationing, transport, black-out and family separations and the accompanying diatribes, often, upon analysis, proving meaningless, upon the dire fate that awaited the Germans – all constituted practically the sum total of the nation's propaganda effort. And they could only be classed as such, because they were translated into German and re-broadcast to Germany by the BBC's overseas network, where it is doubtful if they were heard by anyone but the German monitors of foreign broadcasts. From the outbreak of war, Hitler had declared listening to foreign broadcasts to be treason, punishable by death; though it was not this deterrent which explained their small audience – a far greater deterrent was the dullness of the programmes.

If one were not wildly missing the mark, it seemed quite evident that there existed a policy to do nothing that might goad the Germans to take retaliatory measures of any kind, a policy which was doubtless forced on Whitehall by the French, judging by the Quai d'Orsay's strongly expressed disapproval of a very minor bombing raid carried out by the Royal Air Force on the German island of Sylt.

The censorship at the time was being carried to farcical lengths and gave rise to grave discontent among newspaper men from all over the world, who were prevented from telling Britain's story to their readers without savage cutting of their material or the holding up of it interminably by the censor. One American journalist was kept waiting for two weeks while the censor made up his mind whether or not he would pass an account of a battle-cruiser which the journalist had taken from a four-year-old edition of *Jane's Fighting Ships*, a publication sold in every country in the world, including Germany. Another was refused permission to interview pilots in Lincolnshire, one of whose number had won the first Distinguished Flying Cross of the war.

The Service chiefs were very much in command at this time. Their consternation ran into alarm, when the new First Lord of the Admiralty, Winston Churchill, announced, in one of those magnificently heart-stirring speeches that were to set all Britain gurgling with delight, the number of German U-boats sunk, and added, 'The Royal Navy are carrying out their duties with zest and not without a certain relish'.

Some say that there was collusion in this incident between Churchill and his friend and confidant Beaverbrook. Beaverbrook, Canadian though he was, read the pulse of English men and women precisely, and knew that what the nation wanted was more and more of this frankness and salty humour; and he acted swiftly to bring his tremendous influence and power to bear. First of all he printed the full text of Churchill's speech, and backed it up with editorial comment accusing Chamberlain and the Service chiefs of 'withholding information unnecessarily from the people, our friends and would-be allies'. Soon a campaign for a more sensible and flexible censorship was under way, backed by Beaverbrook's considerable journalistic resources, the outcome of which was a healthy upsurge of public opinion demanding to know what was going on. Other newspapers followed the Beaverbrook lead, the *Daily Mirror* group playing a prominent role. A concerted and slashing attack on Field-Marshal Ironside, Chief of the Imperial General Staff, and General Gort, Commander-in-Chief of the British Expeditionary Forces in France, by Hugh Cudlipp, editor of the *Sunday Pictorial* and that doyen of British journalists William Connor, better known as Cassandra of the *Daily Mirror*, raised an outcry in the House of Commons. But the leaders, in an effort to discipline men who were among the most disciplined members of a highly disciplined profession, decided to make a deterrent example of Connor and Cudlipp, and summarily drafted them into the Army.

In fact, the leaders were in a state of bemusement. Veterans of the ghastly static warfare of World War One, they were bewildered by the *Blitzkrieg* tactics of the Germans. What was needed were commanders of flexibility and vision who could produce counter-tactics which would stop the Germans in their lightning tracks and send them scurrying back the way they had come. Ironically, after the condign punishment handed out to Cudlipp and Connor, it was news, or rather the lack of it, which brought about the changes so desperately needed.

In 1940 the Germans struck at Norway, bringing to an end the Phoney War. British troops were rushed to Norway, and early reports indicated that these forces were incurring heavy losses. Members of Parliament waited until late afternoon to hear a statement from the Prime Minister. All day there had been rumours and speculation, and it was with relief that members heard the message, as they paced the corridors or idled nervously in the smoking rooms, that at last Chamberlain had entered the chamber. When they had hurried to pack the seats and gangways they noticed that the Prime Minister bore signs of nervous strain though he was collected.

He rose and began to make an announcement that units of the Royal Navy were engaged with enemy naval units in 'a fierce battle off the coast of Norway'. He appeared vague about the details, and the House stirred restlessly. Presently a voice from the back benches cried, 'Where?' When Chamberlain made no

46

immediate response, other voices took up the same question, and yet others urged their leader to 'Tell the House!'

The papers he held in his hand trembled as Chamberlain took the impact of the angry and growing storm of protest that was surging round him.

'I can only say,' he said in his unctuous Dissenter-lay-preacher's tones, 'that the battle is being fought in the vicinity of Narvik.' He paused, and then amazingly continued, 'Or it may be Larvik, higher up the coast. . . . I am waiting further reports.'

He sat down to furious shouts of, 'Don't you know or won't you tell us?' and, 'Typical!'

Chamberlain's performance in the House that afternoon marked the beginning of the end of his leadership. A little later, after further disasters, he resigned to make way for Churchill, who, in his first speech to the nation as Prime Minister, told them frankly that all he could offer them was, 'blood, tears, toil and sweat', but promised them, too, that he would never withhold the truth from them, however unpalatable it might be. And, subject to certain unavoidable censorship requirements, this promise he faithfully kept.

It is ironic that Chamberlain who had been so obsessed with the need to speak frankly to the German people should have incurred the wrath of his own friends and countrymen by his inability to appreciate that they deserved similar treatment. If he knew little of war at sea, or land and in the air, it was obvious that he knew less about the war of minds and words that was destined to play an increasingly important role as the war went on.

From the very beginning of his premiership Churchill revealed that he had learned the lessons his

47

predecessor had so painfully disclosed he could not learn. He appointed Duff Cooper to lead the Ministry of Information. It was a significant move, for Duff Cooper was a powerful politician, who as a former First Lord of the Admiralty could have justifiably been expected to receive a higher appointment.

It is interesting to note that the MOI had not been named the Ministry of Propaganda, and that there was never any overt suggestion that its functions were to be anything more than to dispense news. One of its first acts, however, was to take over Campbell Stuart's 'sort of department' and set about – with secret backing – expanding it in every direction.

In the confusion of the Battle for France and the race by the Germans for the Channel ports, the MOI had little it could do but carry out its routine tasks. With the Fall of France, however, Duff Cooper came into his own.

The duty of the Ministry was now clear. It was a two-fold duty; first, it must bend all its efforts to sustain the morale of the British people; second, it must leave no avenue unexplored which might lead to the total demoralisation of the German people.

The evening that the news that France had actually laid down her arms came through, Churchill spoke to the nation. Duff Cooper followed him, making his microphone début as Minister of Information. One might have thought that to try to hold people's attention when they still had the sombre rolling tones of the foremost orator of modern times still ringing in their ears was the height of rashness for any man. But Duff Cooper had not been speaking long when it became apparent that though he could not match the Churchillian bulldog cadences, he, too, was a tough man who knew what he was about. Though not quite in these words, he made it clear that in a way we welcomed what had happened, for now, at least, we knew exactly where we were. With our soldiers restored to us from the Dunkirk beaches, with our factories booming, and the might of the Empire behind us, we would quickly become an impenetrable fortress bristling with armour.

The American journalist William Shirer, who was in Berlin at this time, heard the broadcast in the company of some German journalists. He reported later that these men could not believe that they were hearing aright. Hitler, too, was taken aback when told a little of what Duff Cooper had said, and asked for a full translation of the talk to be urgently prepared for him.

The incident revealed for the first time in concrete form a hint of the great value there could be in playing on the minds of the enemy by confusing him at the same time that morale at home was being boosted. After the war Duff Cooper commented to newspaper men, 'If only the Germans had known that at this moment they could have taken us by telephone!'

As world-wide reaction to Duff Cooper's tough, unrelenting broadcast began to come in, it became increasingly apparent that everyone outside the Axis countries approved, even revelled in, the new 'gloves-off' verbal approach to the war. Anxious not to let a single advantage slip through his fingers, Duff Cooper set up a panel of broadcasters who functioned under the aegis of his Ministry. Prominent among the most successful members of this team were the novelist J B Priestley, whose fireside chats, delivered in a fruity, homely Yorkshire brogue after the Nine O'clock News, no man or woman in the country willingly missed; and the journalist Frank Owen, who later founded the

Army newspapers in the South-East Asia Command. These men, with the greatest star of them all, the Prime Minister, were 'show-stoppers'. Ostensibly they aimed at the Home Front, but they were listened to throughout the world with an eagerness that rivalled that of their more immediate audience. The BBC Overseas Department syndicated them in translation as a stock feature in all their foreign-language series.

Gradually the idea began to take shape – though in whose mind it was first conceived is something of an enigma which official reticence still makes it impossible to solve, though there have been many claims put forward by the admirers of this or that figure – that a definite campaign of 'converting the Germans to the truth of things' should be conducted. If it were to be successful it would have to be organised, and this would require a permanent set-up, a department that could decide policy and control the thousand-and-one details which, when taken in sum, would give the campaign its strength.

Since the beginning of hostilities the BBC's German Service had been 'talking to the Germans', and though there were those who, justifiably, believed that it was not being very effective, it did provide a ready-made channel of communication with the enemy. But the BBC insisted on maintaining its independence. While ready to listen to advice, it, and it alone, would decide whether or not to act upon it.

As happens in all new ventures, there were many varied opinions both about policy and method of operation. By degrees, however, there began to take shape an organisation which would, in obedience to the great British talent for compromise, allow most of the many opinions scope to operate, and which emerged as the Political Warfare Executive.

John Baker White, who was a member of the PWE from its inception – and had previously been connected with Electra House – has said in his book *The Big Lie*:[1] 'It had been evident from the formation of EH (Electra House) that political warfare could not be conducted in a water-tight compartment, and must be co-ordinated with all the other wartime operations. Co-ordination with the military was comparatively simple because political warfare was subordinate to the overall strategic directive, shaping and reshaping itself to conform with current operations. Co-operation with a generally jealous and hostile Ministry of Information was more difficult. Although the Ministry's target was the Home Front, some of its leading officials thought that they should also be responsible for external propaganda. Elements in the Foreign Office had much the same idea. The BBC European Service, the mouthpiece of political warfare, had an uneasy feeling that the new department might try to usurp its jealously guarded independence.'

Baker White also points out that the Ministry of Economic Warfare and its protégé, the Special Operations Executive, which organised subversive activities and resistance in the occupied countries, were involved, too, since 'political and economic warfare had to be closely linked'. So it is not surprising that there was initial frustration and difficulties. However, gradually everything was straightened out, though, as Baker White goes on to say, 'It was a delicate dove-tailing operation. PWE had to fit into the Chiefs of Staff, the Foreign Office, the Ministry of Economic Warfare, the Ministry of Information, SOE and the resistance movement; and after America came into the war, the Psychological Warfare Depart-

[1] Evans Brothers, London, 1955.

ment and the (American) Office of Strategic Services'. The ramifications of PWE were extensive. 'The layout . . . was very complicated,' comments Baker White, 'and rather like the maze at Hampton Court to outsiders, and sometimes even to those who worked in it. I, personally, despite a long time spent on trying to piece it together from the various sources available, must admit complete defeat.'

It is far easier to say what the object of the operations of PWE and its associates was. There was one single aim – to destroy the faith of every single German whether on the home or fighting fronts in Germany's ability to win the war. There were many ways of doing this, and in the account that follows I have selected a number of the highlights of the achievements obtained by those who operated the varying methods. As will be seen, in fact no German was immune from the onslaught of PWE. Bereaved parents, military leaders, Government and Party high officials and rank-and-file, patriotic German workers, and particularly the fighting troops, all came under the pressure of the truth-benders, whether in the form of deceptions, like *The Man Who Never Was* and *I Was Monty's Double*; or rumours, distortion of facts, downright lies disseminated by radio and in leaflets dropped over Germany; or in trying to create confusion among the enemy's administrators by parachuting supplies of food ration cards over the occupied countries (or arranging for their distribution by the Resistance); and so on. And always, the drumming away at the truth in so far as it was such that would add to the despair of the German people.

No holds were barred. The men who mounted the various operations were utterly ruthless. The ethics of an operation might have been vaguely considered in

52

an off-guard moment; but it was for only a fleeting moment.

It was a far far cry from the summer of 1939 when I had been informed that the Foreign Secretary was surprised at my lending my efforts to put forward a suggestion that a secret treaty might be signed with Germany promising Hitler exactly what an open treaty signed with the Russians promised them, and he begged to remind me that such an arrangement 'just wasn't cricket'. I doubt whether any of the long list of brilliant men who undertook to destroy Germany by falsehood ever once mentioned, or even thought of, the rules of cricket while they were doing it.

# 4 : Der Chef

IN THE ONE or two accounts that have been published dealing with various activities of the truth-benders, the terms *Political Warfare* and *Psychological Warfare* have been used with such apparent impartiality that the uninitiated could be excused if he fell into some confusion. In fact, all the activities which concentrated on trying to undermine the morale of the Germans either by ramming home the Great Truth or the Big Lie or any other kind of deception was basically psychological in nature. I intend, therefore, from this point on to avoid, as far as I can, mention of Political Warfare Executive and Psychological Warfare Department.

Some of the branches of the truth-bending organisation were sited in London, but the chief centre of their activities was the Stately Home of the Duke of Bedford. At Woburn Abbey and in nearby villages on the Bedford estate, a collection of brilliant men who had no compunction about the ethics of what they were doing conceived their ideas and put them into action, often with a ruthlessness and utter lack of human feeling which can still often shock, in retrospect, their most ardent supporters. Among the most successful of all the truth-benders was the internationally famous former correspondent of the *Daily Express*, Sefton Delmer.

Before the war, Delmer had been Lord Beaver-brook's Man-in-Germany. Such was his status as a foreign correspondent that he had been invited by Hitler to travel with him and his entourage round Germany. He had come to know the German leaders well, and had made a close study of the club-footed Josef Goebbels, Hitler's own truth-bender *sans pareil* (almost). He had a deep and clear insight into the German Minister of Propaganda's mind and person-ality, and from long association with Germany, he had an appreciation of the German character without equal among Englishmen. He had watched the rise and growth of the Nazi régime, and he hated every-thing about it. Fortunately, these qualities were recognised by the men in the psychological warfare corridors of power.

In July 1940, Duff Cooper, the new Minister of Information, started Delmer on the path which he was to tread so brilliantly until the end of the war, by inviting him to join the band of BBC broadcasters to Germany. By a rare coincidence, his first appearance before the microphone was scheduled for the evening of 19th July, the evening which Hitler had chosen to address a meeting of the Reichstag to celebrate his victory over France and at the same time make his 'final peace offer' to Britain.

It was decided that Delmer should reply to Hitler. From the time that the Führer finished speaking, to the time that he himself went on the air, he had only an hour in which to prepare what he was going to say. His reaction was to reject Hitler's peace offer, and, with the concurrence of the BBC, this he prepared to do. His German was flawless; he was the master of the telling phrase, the nice nuance, in that language no less than in his own.

'Let me tell you,' he said, addressing himself directly to Hitler, 'what we here in Britain think of this appeal of yours to what you are pleased to call our reason and commonsense. Herr Führer and Reichskanzler, we hurl it right back at you, right in your evil-smelling teeth.'

As a broadcast, it would have been a *tour de force* at any time. In this special context it was that, and more. In his tremendous study, *The Rise and Fall of the Third Reich*,[1] William Shirer, the American radio commentator, has described its effect on 'Junior officers of the High Command and officials from various Ministries' who were present when he listened to Delmer's broadcast. 'Their faces fell. They could not believe their ears. "Can you make it out?" one of them shouted to me. He seemed dazed. "Can you understand these British fools?" he continued to bellow. "To turn down peace now? They're crazy!" '

But the broadcast also had its repercussions in England. In *Their Finest Hour*,[2] Churchill, referring to the Government's plans to reply to Hitler – the Foreign Secretary was to 'brush aside Hitler's summons to capitulate to his will' – wrote: 'In fact, however, the rejection of any idea of a parley had already been given by the BBC without any prompting from His Majesty's Government, as soon as Hitler's speech was heard over the radio.'

Delmer was attacked in the House of Commons by the Socialist MP for Ipswich, Richard Stokes, who demanded to know how the Government had permitted Delmer, 'a person of no importance, to deliver an answer to Hitler less than two hours after the Chancellor had spoken. I think it entirely wrong that

[1] Secker and Warburg, London, 1960, p. 755.
[2] Cassell, London: 1949, p. 218.

a speech broadcast in Germany at six o'clock should not first have had consideration from responsible people. . . .'

Duff Cooper told the House, however, that the Cabinet fully approved of Delmer's broadcast. Hitler did not, and added this name to the list of Englishmen to be liquidated when the Germans occupied Britain.

A few weeks later, Delmer was asked by Leonard Ingrams, chief of the Political Warfare Executive, a former Oxford Half-Blue and a banker by profession (and something of a financial wizard), if he would consider resigning from the *Daily Express* and joining the German broadcasts unit on a full-time basis. Delmer agreed, but the Security authorities, for reasons best known to themselves, refused to give him clearance. Much valuable time was lost before Security were eventually persuaded to change their minds, and Delmer was introduced to Woburn Abbey.

For his active mind and, despite his sixteen-stone-plus, his energetic body, his work was quite inadequate. He was on the point of resigning when Ingrams offered him another job; one in which all his gifts were brought into play and in which he was to make a tremendous contribution to the psychological war-effort.

For some time PWE maintained two units broadcasting from special transmitters situated in England, though the 'stations' tried to make the Germans believe that they were Resistance organisations broadcasting over secret transmitters inside Germany. Recently one of these units had had to disband owing to the illness of its chief operator. The other was manned by a group of German Marxists, who operated it under the kindly supervision of Richard Crossman, though he had no control over either the matter or method of broadcasting. The authorities believed that this station ought to be counter-balanced by a Right-wing group, and proposed that Delmer should take charge of it. He would have full control; the Germans who worked for him would carry out his instructions; and he alone would decide the content and method of each broadcast. The Germans had recently launched a Right-wing freedom station broadcasting in English, which they called The Workers' Challenge. Directed to the British working man, it used foul language, employing every tabu four-letter word with stunning frequency, obviously in the belief that by doing so they would make contact easier with the workers.

'Old ladies in Eastbourne and Torquay are listening to it avidly,' Ingrams told Delmer. 'They enjoy counting the F's and the B's. Well, my Minister thinks we should reply in kind.'

Delmer accepted the offer with alacrity, and before long he established his unit in a house in the village of Aspley Guise, on the Bedford estate, his plan for organising it approved by the authorities. This plan, in general terms, differed from all the other so-called Freedom stations and the BBC, which contented themselves in urging the Germans to rise against Hitler. Delmer's idea was to undermine Hitler, not by opposing him, as the other stations did, but by pretending to support him and the war. He aimed to appeal to what he called the 'inner pig-dog' inside every German, and to do so 'in the name of his highest patriotic ideals. Give him a reason for doing what he would like to do from patriotic self-interest, talk to him about his Führer and his Fatherland and all that sort of thing, and at the same time inject some item of news into his mind which will make him think, and, if possible, act, in a way that is contrary to the efficient conduct of Hitler's war.'

It was on this basis that Delmer's first black radio was operated throughout its long existence. It also broke new ground in its presentation. 'I would try to make the German listener believe that he was eavesdropping on a radio talk not meant for his ears. As he twiddled the knobs on his set, he would suddenly find himself tuned in to what sounded like the signals traffic of a clandestine military organisation sending cyphered instructions to its secret cells all over occupied Europe.' When there was no cyphered material awaiting transmission 'a die-hard of the old Prussian school' would give the members of this imaginary organisation his outspoken views on what was happening in Germany and beyond. But always there would be apparent support for the Führer and the Fatherland.

'The station, in fact,' Delmer has remarked, 'would seek to be a nightly demonstration of a growing split between the conservative elements of the Army and the radicals of the Nazi Party.'

The station was called *Gustav Siegfried Eins* – the German signaller's equivalent of GSI; the nameless commentator was known simply as *Der Chef*, the Chief, who was, in fact, a Corporal seconded from the Pioneer Corps.

*Gustav Siegfried Eins* broadcast for the first time on the evening of 23rd May 1941. Delmer was not really ready, but just twelve days earlier Rudolf Hess, Hitler's deputy, had suddenly and somewhat unexpectedly dropped out of the Scottish skies. For some still not entirely explicable reason, Churchill had refused to allow the BBC to exploit fully this bizarre incident. Der Chef, on the other hand, suffered no such restrictions, and in those twelve days it had become progressively clearer that he would have to intervene.

This first broadcast set the pattern for all that were to follow. For three-quarters of a minute, Der Chef repeated his call-sign – Gustav Siegfried Eins – and then began to announce some coded instructions to various other cells in his organisation. The first was, 'Here is Gustav Siegfried Eins calling Gustav Siegfried 18, here is a message for Gustav Siegfried 18.'

The message was in a fairly simple code which, Delmer knew, would be easily broken by the German secret service. When this had been done, he was hopeful that 'it would produce quite an acceptable flurry in the Gestapo dove-cotes all over Germany', for it said, 'Willy meet Jochen Friday row five parquet stalls second performance Union Theatre.' As there were several hundred theatres of this name scattered throughout Germany, and though the German radio experts would quickly discover that Gustav Siegfried Eins was situated on British territory, the Gestapo would probably believe that Willy and Jochen were British agents and would send their own men to visit every Union Theatre in the country to try to catch them.

When Der Chef had completed his message, he began his talk. To make it seem that Gustav Siegfried Eins had been broadcasting for some time, he said that he was answering questions that had been sent to him after his last broadcast, when he had warned his listeners that Hess was about to do something stupid. He had ordered his comrades to lie low during the investigation which would inevitably follow Hess's flight from Germany, and he himself had remained silent for the same reason. Now he believed the danger had passed and here he was again.

'First, let's get this straight,' he said, 'this fellow is by no means the worst of the lot. He was a good comrade of ours in the days of the Free Corps. But like the rest of this clique of cranks, megalomaniacs, string-pullers and parlour Bolsheviks who call themselves our leaders, he simply has no nerves for a crisis. As soon as he learns a little of the darker side of the developments that lie ahead, what happens? He loses his head completely, packs himself a satchel of hormone pills and a white flag, and flies off to throw himself and us on the mercy of that flat-footed bastard of a drunken old Jew, Churchill. And he overlooks completely that he is the bearer of the Reich's most precious secrets, all of which the ***** British will now suck out of him as easily as if he were a bottle of Berlin White-beer. I must, however, deny one thing that some of the lick-spittles in the Führer's headquarters are putting around, namely, that the fellow flew to Britain on the Führer's orders. That I am convinced is quite out of the question. The Führer would never have authorised a man with such an intimate knowledge of our operational plans to go into enemy country. And that is proved, too, by the drastic way the Führer is dealing with those who have, by their negligence, permitted this grave blow against the future of our Fatherland to be struck, namely, the Security snoopers, who, if they had been anywhere near as good as they say they are, would have stopped the poor idiot in time. Unfortunately, however, that supreme ****** of a Reich's Security Chief, to get himself out of the mess, has seen fit to arrest a number of men – leaders of industry, leaders of the Abwehr – true German patriots, all of them, men of the deepest national devotion and fatherland-loyalty, men whose one fault was that they misjudged the nerve strength of this so-called deputy leader and told him, in the last days of April, of their grave misgivings, which, owing to the hedge of liars and lick-spittle sycophants that surround him, they had been unable to place before the Führer himself.'

A list of the names of those arrested followed, and the amazing thing was, that although the list was pure invention, several of the men Delmer put in it had actually been arrested. Equally fortuitous was the fact that though Delmer could have no inkling of it when he made Der Chef refer to 'the darker side of the developments that lie ahead', Hitler was on the point of launching *Operation Barbarossa*, the Nazi invasion of Russia.

Another typical, though deliberate touch, was the reference to 'that flat-footed bastard of a drunken old Jew'. This was the phrase which roused Sir Stafford Cripps's angry retort, when given a transcript to read, that, 'If we have to resort to this sort of thing to win the war, I'd rather we lost it.' But psychologically it was unassailable. No German listening to such words would ever believe that official British propagandists would dare to describe the country's leader in those terms; *ergo*, the station must be anti-British Government, to say the least, even if one might occasionally doubt that it was all it claimed to be.

After this first effort, *Gustav Siegfried Eins* went from strength to strength, and this was due almost as much to the talks that Delmer very carefully selected as to Delmer's direction. Der Chef can now be identified as Corporal Paul Sanders, who was, in fact, a Berliner and a writer of detective stories. Sickened by the Nazi Party's persecution of the Jews, in 1938 he had left Germany and come to Britain, and immediately war had broken out, had enlisted in the British Army. Later, he offered to parachute back into Germany as an SOE agent, which was how he was known to Leonard Ingrams, who introduced him to Delmer.

Another of GSI's team was Johannes Reinholz, a German journalist, who fled to England to protect his Jewish wife. From the beginning of the Nazi era, Reinholz had worked against Hitler. It was Reinholz who wrote most of Der Chef's talks – which Delmer had done at the beginning – thus releasing Delmer to devote himself to plotting GSI's exploits.

The third man in the team was the former German Socialist leader Max Braun, who had led the opposition to Hitler in the Saar. He was useful to Delmer for his many contacts in Germany and equally because he had a supreme gift for interpreting the German news. Two other men completed the team – Albrecht Ernst and Alexander Maass, whom Delmer had known in the International Brigade that had fought in Spain during the Civil War. With the help of these five men led by Delmer *Gustav Siegfried Eins* played an outstanding role on the psychological war-front.

The Germans had their own star performers, the counterparts of our J B Priestley, Quentin Reynolds and others, and the chief of them was undoubtedly Hans Fritzsche, who gave a weekly pep-talk to the nation over the Deutschlandsender. It was Richard Crossman's idea – Crossman was director of what may be termed White propaganda at Woburn – that Delmer should listen to Fritzsche's talks and an hour-and-a-half later reply to them over the BBC German service.

Delmer was on the point of setting out for London to make the first of his attacks on Fritzsche on 21st June 1941, when he was summoned to a conference at the Abbey, which had been called to reveal to the propagandists that British Intelligence had discovered that Hitler was about to attack Russia. During the proceedings Delmer was asked what line Der Chef would take.

'Der Chef is all for Hitler and his war on the Bolsheviks,' Delmer replied, somewhat to the surprised horror of those who had not heard of Der Chef. 'He will insist that the Führer combines his anti-British crusade against Soviet Russia with a clearing-up campaign against the Bolsheviks at home, the Bolsheviks, that is, of the National Socialist German Workers Party. . . . Der Chef has collected a great deal of astonishing material about these Bolsheviks which he will bring to the attention of the Führer.'

It was, in fact, the German-Russian war that firmly established Der Chef. He was at his most eloquent as he raved against the Bolsheviks in Russia and the Communists in the Nazi Party. Each time the German forces suffered a set-back he blamed it on the 'Party Bolsheviks' – the German term is *Parteikommune*. 'While our brave soldiers are freezing to death in Russia because of the corruption of this Parteikommune crowd,' he exclaimed, 'who delayed getting the Army's winter clothing ready in time because they were out for bigger profit, these same traitorous swine are having a wonderful time feathering their nests in the soft-job billets far from danger and privation.'

The motive behind this line of attack was to make the German man-in-the-street ask himself, 'Why should I put up with this when those Party swine can get out of it all?' The Party officials were Delmer's main target, and by attacking them Delmer hoped to counteract in some degree the extremely impressive job that Goebbels and his underlings were doing in keeping German morale up and urging the Germans on to even greater efforts and to accept even greater sacrifices.

Lurid stories were invented purporting to disclose how high-ranking Nazi officials – not the leaders, because they were the constant butt of other propagandists – used the knowledge they gleaned in their Party jobs and from their Party connections to gain privileges for themselves at the expense of the national economy. Once, for example, Der Chef used a whole talk to describe how the wives of some high officials in Holstein, whom he named, had learned from their husbands that soon there would be no textiles left in Germany and had immediately rushed to a department store and bought all the textiles to which they were entitled on their clothes ration. He also exposed the sexual aberrations (invented) in great detail of other officials and their wives.

At the beginning of his career, Der Chef dealt largely with inventions. Later, however, he began to profit from rumours that were being constantly circulated in such neutral centres as Berne, Zürich, Madrid and Lisbon, where Allies and enemy alike maintained listening posts.

The names and addresses used by Der Chef were all genuine. Max Braun organised a file for the news items, the births, deaths and marriages announcements and the small advertisements in German newspapers. If Der Chef needed a butcher from Koblenz or an ironmonger from Wiesbaden, he consulted Max's file. Newspaper articles were also a fertile source of inspiration to him.

Perhaps the most valuable source of all information for Der Chef in his efforts to reach and impress – and depress – the ordinary Germans were the recordings that were made by eavesdropping – by means of concealed microphones – on German prisoners of war. Unaware that they could be overheard the prisoners had few inhibitions about letting down their hair in a good, genuine grouse. From these conversations, he not only gained material for the subject-matter of his broadcasts, but kept abreast of all the latest slang.

Then there were the letters intercepted by British Postal Censorship. From the correspondence of the American wife of a Cologne industrialist, to her friend in Nevada, which described the wonderful parties given by the young Nazi Mayor Winkelkampner and Gauleiter Grohe which she and her husband attended and at which there were always masses of food that was strictly rationed for ordinary Germans, Der Chef concocted a wonderful tirade against Party officials who, while requiring others to keep the law, broke it flagrantly themselves.

Within a short time Der Chef was firmly established, making his nightly contact with his 'organisation' and always ready with a story showing-up misdemeanour of the men in power which could not fail to exacerbate the nervous strain under which the majority of ordinary Germans existed. Soon information began to trickle back of the effect that the broadcasts were having on those who were listening to them and on those to whom the listeners passed on what they heard.

The value of *Gustav Siegfried Eins* was undoubted, yet strangely enough the Services in Britain were slow to recognise it. The first to do so was the Admiralty, and this was chiefly due to a meeting which Delmer had with Admiral Godfrey, and which had been arranged for him by his friend Ian Fleming way back in 1939. Almost as soon as he heard of GSI's existence and its work, Admiral Godfrey, who was Director of Naval Intelligence, recognised how useful the organisation could be in misleading German Naval Intelligence. As a result, he established a Propaganda Section whose function was to organise a psychological attack on German crews, and put it over with the help of GSI.

Der Chef continued to function until the end of October 1943. There is no doubt that he would have gone on much longer had it not been for the fact that early in 1942 Delmer had started on two other projects of a similar nature, but more specific in aim.

Shortly before the end of 1942, the Admiralty embarked upon an all-out effort to clear the seas of U-boats. New weapons for detecting and destroying them had been produced and were so effective that sailing in a U-boat had become a very hazardous pursuit indeed. At the same time it was suggested that a simultaneous psychological attack would make the campaign doubly effective. In addition it was thought that if the morale of the German Navy cracked, the rot would spread to the Wehrmacht and the Luftwaffe.

In order to promote the Black programme, the Admiralty asked Delmer if he would extend the scope of GSI for this purpose, by introducing into it a black news bulletin, i.e. a bulletin in which true and bent-true items would be mixed. Such a bulletin had been one of Delmer's dreams for some time, but he had not been able to put it into effect, because it did not fit in with the image of Der Chef.

In fact, Delmer had made one attempt to launch a black news bulletin over a station he had called *Wehrmachtsender Nord*, but had soon abandoned it because the programme had had to be pre-recorded, which had destroyed the spontaneity which all news must have, and which broadcast news can only achieve if transmitted live. In view of this experience, Delmer told the Admiralty that he would be pleased to co-operate but only if facilities could be obtained for it to be sent out live. If this permission were obtained, then, he said, they could set up a fake forces broadcast on the lines of the genuine German forces stations in Yugoslavia and Poland.

As luck would have it, PWE had recently built a powerful medium-wave transmitter with which it was intended to broadcast on German wavelengths and by its sheer power to drown the German stations and assert its own voice. At the moment, however, the transmitter had been loaned to the BBC, and its studios at Molton Bryan, near Woburn, were unused. Delmer proposed that these studios could be used, and after some resistance from the BBC, who were ultimately overruled, the first black station to broadcast live news bulletins came into being. It was called Atlantiksender, and opened on 5th February 1943.

The launching of Atlantiksender necessitated increasing Delmer's staff, and here he was very fortunate in obtaining the services of Clifton Child, a young Manchester education officer, as his chief intelligence expert and C E Stevens, an Ancient History lecturer at Oxford, as Child's assistant. They were a brilliant team, for, as Delmer says, 'Child had an almost supernatural genius for ferreting German news from the most unpromising sources, while Stevens was a walking encyclopaedia. He carried the most abstruse facts and statistics in his head'.

As his deputy in running Atlantiksender, Delmer secured Karl Robson, who had been a newspaper correspondent in Berlin right up to 3rd September 1939, and spoke German well. He was a first-class sub-editor, and being a journalist was able to appreciate Delmer's main requirement of 'easily understood colloquial German in short sentences'.

69

In addition to these men at the top, Atlantiksender also drew on the German forces themselves for its staff. Among the prisoners taken in the Atlantic and North Africa were always a number of genuine anti-Hitler sailors, soldiers and airmen, who asked only for an opportunity to help bring about his overthrow, no matter how insignificant their personal contribution might be. 'From the ranks of these men,' Delmer has said, 'I selected some of my ablest fellow workers.'

By a great stroke of good fortune, Delmer was able to obtain a Hellschreiber. A Hellschreiber was a German wireless teleprinter machine used by Goebbels for disseminating the news to all the newspapers in Germany and the German-occupied territories. Atlantiksender was, therefore, on a par with any German radio station when it came to receiving the very latest news approved for public consumption by the Ministry of Propaganda and Public Enlightenment. Very often Atlantiksender broadcast news items culled from this source before any genuine German station did. As may be imagined, this ability greatly enhanced the authentic character of Atlantiksender and so increased the deception in the minds of ordinary German troops who could not know that the transmitter actually stood on British territory.

All the special jargon which Goebbels had introduced, for example Terror Raids for RAF air raids and Terror Flyers for their crews, were also used in Atlantiksender's bulletins. Like other German stations, Atlantiksender interrupted their own broadcasts whenever Hitler or Goebbels spoke over the German wireless, and put out their speeches. In fact every trick was used to give the station a genuine German character.

The object of Atlantiksender was to destroy the morale of the German forces as quickly as possible, and it sought to do so by a cunning mixture of true news and bent news. For example, to attract German workers back to work after particularly heavy air raids, Goebbels announced that a special air-raid bonus of chocolate and food was being distributed to works canteens. Atlantiksender broadcast this news, but added that this special chocolate and food had been injected with stimulant drugs which would give the tired workers more energy. When it became known that bombed-out families in Hamburg were being evacuated to the Eastern territories, Atlantiksender added the additional information that epidemics of cholera and typhus had broken out in Poland and Slovakia. No holds barred, Atlantiksender announced that similar epidemics had broken out in the special evacuee children's camp, known as KLV.

This was not just a bald announcement, but put over in a much more subtle fashion. 'Dr Conti, the Reichsführer for Physicians, has congratulated the medical officers at the KLV camps in the Gau Wartheland for the selfless devotion with which they are fighting the diphtheria epidemic among the children in their care. He has expressed his satisfaction at their success in overcoming the tragic lack of medicaments, and reducing deaths by an average of sixty a week.'

One can imagine the effect such news might have on any German soldier father who had children in a KLV in Gau Wartheland, or in any other children's camp, or had in bombed cities families who might be evacuated to places where typhus and cholera were raging. The constant concern of Atlantiksender was to keep the soldier at the Front, the sailor at sea, the airman on his foreign airfield, separated by hundreds of miles and bad communications, in a perpetual state of apprehension about the welfare of his family.

Another attempt to do this was made by broadcasting the names of streets bombed in the raids of the previous evening, and reminding the troops that if the house in which their family lived had been hit they could apply for compassionate leave. Yet another line was to sow unhappiness among married and engaged men by reporting divorce cases and broadcasting stories which suggested that many wives and sweethearts were being unfaithful while husbands and lovers were away from home.

But Atlantiksender ranged even more widely than the forces. Stevens, who had good contacts in several government departments, obtained a Ministry of Economic Warfare's Black List of neutral industries that were suspected of trading with Germany. Names from this list and the suspected crime were broadcast and had the effect of making these firms stop their legitimate but frowned-upon business.

In a very short time Delmer received indications – chiefly through prisoners of war – of the effect Atlantiksender was having on German troops' morale. Atlantiksender was transmitted on short waves, and to increase the effect, it was decided to open a similar station on medium waves; and so the Soldatensender Calais came into being. This station worked on identical lines and before very long was proving its worth.

The setting up of the Soldatensender had not been easy, for Delmer encountered strong opposition in some quarters, which was summed up by Sir Ivone Kirkpatrick, who represented the European Service of the BBC in the PWE.

'Black is all right on short wave,' he declared. 'But

if you get on medium wave with all your lies and distortions, you will undermine the whole currency value of British propaganda as a purveyor of truth.'

The Service ministries, however, took a different view. The time had come when a more rapid softening-up of the German troops was needed, and this, it was believed, Auntie BBC could not do. Firmest support for Delmer came from Major-General Dallas Brooks, deputy director-general of PWE in the absence of Robert Bruce Lockhart, the director-general, who, nevertheless, warned Delmer when permission for the establishment of Soldatensender had been given, 'I'm taking a big gamble on this, Tone. If you make a mess of things it will be my head that rolls in the sand.'

From its very first broadcast on 24th October 1943 Delmer's new baby was a brilliant success. Even Kirkpatrick graciously admitted it, though he gave it as his opinion that, with his present staff, Delmer would be unable to maintain the initial impact.

This impact was not only appreciated at home. In his diary for 28th November 1943, Josef Goebbels noted, 'In the evening the so-called Soldatensender Calais, which evidently originates in England and uses the same wave-lengths as Radio Deutschland – when the latter is out during their air-raids – gave us something to worry about. The station does a very clever job of propaganda and from what is put on the air, one can gather that the English know exactly what they have destroyed in Berlin and what they have not.'

The Bavarian Ministry of the Interior, six months after Soldatensender's first transmission, was becoming extremely apprehensive of its effect on the population. On 16th March 1944, it sent a minute to SS Obergruppenführer and General of Police, Freiherr von Eberstein (Himmler's Chief of Security Police in

Munich) which began: 'Since October 1943 increasingly frequent references are being made by the population to the transmissions of the radio station which calls itself Soldatensender Calais and concerning whose nationality people are not clear. The chief effect of the station's news transmissions, which have been described as psychologically excellent, emerges from its practice of giving absolutely unexceptionable information which has also been carried verbatim in the German News Service and mixing in with it a number of isolated, more or less tendentious items. This has caused large portions of the population to believe that Soldatensender Calais is a German station, perhaps one of the many Soldatensender started up in the occupied territories also without anything about them being officially communicated to the population. That the reports of the Soldatensender Calais often have a sharpness otherwise nowhere to be found in the German News Service is in some cases explained by the population on the following lines: "After all they cannot present the soldier at the front with the same propaganda as they sell us at home. They have to be more honest with the soldiers at the front".'

Apparently, Munich radio had carried programmes for the ousted Mussolini's Salo Republic. These broadcasts, the minute continues, 'caused the greatest indignation among listeners here, and forces them to dial other stations in order not to lose their evening's entertainment. They twiddle and find the Soldatensender Calais, which comes through with extraordinary power, and holds the population with its news service. . . .'

The object of Soldatensender Calais was to suggest to the Germans that in the West there was in reality another phoney war, though with slight differences. Delmer called it a 'Sitzkrieg' in which all military effort was futile and dangerous. It was dangerous, he said, for the troops to show themselves militarily efficient, for efficient units were sent to the Eastern Front. It was this front, and not the West, which the High Command regarded as the most important; all reinforcements and supplies were being sent there while the West remained neglected. This theme was plugged in dozens of news items, true and truth-bent.

(How successful the Soldatensender was was clearly illustrated when the High Command instructed unit commanders in the West to lecture their men about the Poison Transmitter Calais.)

In keeping with the main objective, Soldatensender also tried to lower the troops' morale in the West even further by putting out that the troops in Russia had no hope of resisting the Red forces successfully, for the Americans were supplying the Russians with their very latest weapons. It described one of these as a phosphorous shell which could penetrate practically anything and when it burst, burnt up everything within range. It was these shells, Soldatensender proclaimed, that were responsible for Germany's latest defeats in Russia.

The obvious success which Soldatensender achieved from the very beginning made a great impression on the Allied Service chiefs, American as well as British, and it was included in the preparatory plans for the invasion of Normandy. Delmer now received all the aid he required, for if the morale of the German troops who would oppose the invasion forces could be seriously undermined, it was logical to expect that their resistance would be that much weaker.

The Americans had made preparations for waging

psychological warfare some months before Pearl Harbor. In November 1940, President Roosevelt had sent Colonel 'Big Bill' Donovan on a fact-finding tour of the major war fronts. On a visit to Britain the Colonel was shown the workings of PWE and was clearly impressed, for in July 1941, three months after his return from his tour, Donovan was appointed Co-ordinator of Defence Information, and at once began the organisation of a political warfare department, and by the time Pearl Harbor occurred he had made such strides in this direction, that only a short period elapsed before America became active on the psychological warfare front.

Delmer's black propaganda efforts were not all confined to radio. In his 'Overlord' office on the top floor of Bush House, in the Strand, London, he received many secret visitors, officers of the various resistance movements in the occupied countries – French, Dutch, Belgians, Poles, Americans, Danes, Norwegians, British. They had been sent to see him by SOE and SOE's American counterpart, the OSS, before returning to The Field, so that he could explain to them how his unit might help them.

One point he stressed to them above all others: when they killed a German they should, whenever possible, make it appear that the killer had been a German. In this way they could help foster the notion in the minds of the Gestapo and other security forces that a German underground movement existed also. For his part, he could show them all kinds of tricks for deceiving the German troops which would help his role as the destroyer of German morale.

He showed them how to write letters containing rumours and false information, then tear them up and scatter them where a German soldier was likely to find them. He also introduced them to a leaflet which, he hoped, would encourage German troops to desert to Switzerland or Sweden. It was a forgery of the propaganda leaflet produced by the Wehrmacht, called *Information for the Troops*, and referred to the problem of the increasing number of desertions which faced the Field Security Police. Copies of it, he said, dropped where a German officer could have dropped it and where it was likely to be picked up by a German soldier would have more chances of success than if it were scattered in thousands over occupied areas.

Another was a poster which appeared to have been issued by the German Security Police. It contained a badly printed picture of a German soldier with his description and the information that he was wanted for murder. He was such a bad character that he should be taken alive or dead. In other words, it invited fellow Germans and Norwegians – it was printed in Norwegian as well – to kill Germans. It was, in fact, a highly effective piece of propaganda.

Then there was a sticker headed 'Six weeks in dock', which explained how to sabotage a U-boat's diesel engines. The Norwegian resistance had first used it, sticking it up round the U-boat pens in Bergen and Trondhjem. Its object was not so much to encourage U-boat crews to sabotage their ships as to worry the Field Security Police. The Poles also made good use of them at Golynin, and the French at St Nazaire and L'orient.

One of Delmer's efforts rather backfired. This was a handbook, prepared for him by Dr J T McCurdy, lecturer in mental illness at Cambridge University, which explained symptoms which could be faked so well that a doctor would be deceived into granting sick-leave. In other words, it was a *Handbook for Malingerers*. The Germans thought so highly of it as a propaganda weapon that they had it translated into English, and introduced it to the British and American troops.

Two other 'weapons' illustrate nicely how thoroughly PWD – the Psychological Warfare Division – interpreted 'no holds barred'. When a German soldier died in hospital, the doctor sent a telegram *en clair*, by radio, to the local Party official asking him to break the news to the dead man's parents and relatives. PWD was able to intercept these telegrams, which gave the name of the dead man, the address of his relatives, and the name of the hospital.

Armed with this information, a letter was written in longhand on notepaper headed with the name of the hospital. The writer said he was a friend of the deceased, and he described how, right up to his death, the dead man had expressed his faith in the Führer's leadership and in ultimate victory. He then went on to say that the dead man had mentioned a small possession, a ring, a watch or a gold crucifix – which he wanted his relatives to have as a memento. It had been sent to such and such a Party official who would hand it over in person.

When sufficient time had passed for the delivery of the letter, Soldatensender then went into the attack. One of Delmer's men, Sepp Obermeyer, roundly accused the corpse-robbers who did not hesitate to steal the possessions of men who had given their lives for their country.

As a variation on this theme, the 'friend' would sometimes tell the parents that their son had not died of his wounds, but of a lethal injection administered by a doctor. The doctor had decided that the man could not recover, and his bed was urgently needed for another wounded man.

The second 'weapon' also involved the death of a soldier. Delmer discovered that the prisoner-of-war postal censorship was receiving letters from parents of sons who were missing, although they had been told that there was no trace of them in the West. These letters from men and women, who refused to accept that their sons were probably dead, contained all the family news and gossip.

Taking some of these letters, Delmer arranged for replies to be sent, telling the parents not to make any further inquiries about the whereabouts of their son. Along with other comrades, he was safe and well in a neutral country, and when the war was over he would send for them. The letter concluded, 'Please tell no one about this letter.' (The letters were posted inside Germany.)

Delmer believed that the parents would not be able to keep the news to themselves, and thus the idea that German soldiers were successfully deserting to neutral countries would spread, and encourage others to do likewise.

Heartless, cruel, cynical all such tricks undoubtedly were. But if the ends ever justified the means, this certainly applied in unrestricted warfare.

Delmer also had a hand in the production of the leaflets dropped in their millions over Germany and the occupied territories. As I have mentioned, a special squadron of Flying Fortresses was set aside purely to carry out leaflet raids. Gone were the days when the leaflets were pushed through a chute in the floor of a Wellington bomber.

By October 1943, thanks to the ingenuity of a young American Air Force captain, James Monroe, the method of delivery had become much more sophisticated. He had invented a leaflet bomb – a cylinder of laminated wax paper, five feet long and one-and-a-half feet in diameter, which would hold 80,000 leaflets. When they descended to a height of 1000 feet an automatic fuse opened the bomb and the leaflets were released.

In his view, the most successful leaflets concocted by Delmer were those which he called *News for the Troops*. With the help of a team of expert editors and news writers, provided by SHAEF's Psychological Warfare Division and working under his instructions, Delmer produced a daily 'newspaper' which was delivered night after night over the German lines in France and Belgium, and deep into Germany. It was a tremendous achievement, for *News for the Troops* was delivered on 345 consecutive nights. An average of two million copies of each number was printed on the presses of the Home Counties Newspapers at Luton, Bedfordshire.

And all the time that he was engaged on these and other deceptions, Delmer worked with unabated energy on the Soldatensender's programmes and other black radio projects. His main objective was still to drive home to the German troops in the West that the High Command accorded them only second priority, and by this and other means to destroy their morale.

In volume 2 of his autobiography, *Black Boomerang*, he has given several examples of the kind of item which Soldatensender broadcast.

'Further tank forces from the Command of C-in-C West will shortly follow the SS Panzer divisions Hohenstanfen and Frundsberg to the

Eastern Front. Drafts are also being sent from West units hitherto considered below the standard needed for the Eastern front. They are being sent to reinforce the Rumanian sector where our long-distance air reconnaissance reports heavy Russian troop concentrations, indicating the imminence of a new Russian offensive.'

\*　　\*　　\*　　\*　　\*

'A new swindle racket by platform vendors on Cologne main station is claiming numerous victims among Wehrmacht personnel in the German transports now passing through Cologne on their way from the West to the East Front. Just before the train is due to depart the vendors offer the comrades bottles of Eau de Cologne at much reduced prices. But though these bottles contain genuine Cologne water it is not the famous Cologne perfume but only Cologne tap-water.'

\*　　\*　　\*　　\*　　\*

After a group of American Mustang fighters had made an attack on a château thought to be housing a German staff HQ, Delmer told the troops:

'Field-Marshal Rommel has once more escaped an attempt to ambush and kill him. This morning he was due to visit Château Lebiex. At the last minute he changed his mind and cancelled the inspection. But at nine-thirty am, ten minutes after his party had been scheduled to arrive, a flight of enemy Mustangs dived out of the clouds onto the château and shot it up with rockets. The château and the entire staff HQ were destroyed.'

*　　*　　*　　*　　*

The failure of the police to find the French mass-murderer Dr Marcel Petiot was used to drive home the idea that it was quite safe for troops to desert. Thus:

'The increase in acts of sabotage committed by French guerillas disguised in Waffen SS uniforms has led to the issue of a new order by the chief of the military government in France, Dr Michel. It lays down that all directives must in future be signed with the full name. In several cases, members of the French underground have succeeded in obtaining Waffen SS uniforms by producing orders with illegible signatures. The habit of signing orders illegibly has increased recently, since it became known that French organisations are collecting the names of officials of the occupying authorities and smuggling them abroad to have them added to the list of war criminals.'

*　　*　　*　　*　　*

Or to encourage malingering:

'. . . Oberstammführer Schmutzler owes his temporary laming to an old and infallible prescription. He tied a rubber eraser to the hollow of his knee at night so that it pressed hard against the nerve until the symptoms of genuine lameness were manifested, thus procuring his release from the Army.'

On D-Day, 6th June 1944, the *News for the Troops* probably reached its zenith. Preparations for the great day had been made well in advance, and a mock-up of the paper waited to be rolled off the presses as soon as the announcement of invasion had been made. Tied to it were the operations of Soldatensender. The main objective, irrespective of whether our forces had succeeded in landing or had been pushed back into the sea, was to make the German troops believe that their defences had been penetrated in several places, and that they would be wise to surrender.

Immediately Goebbels's news-agency DNB announced the invasion, Soldatensender almost simultaneously declared, 'The enemy is landing in force from the air and from the sea. The Atlantic Wall is penetrated in several places. The Command has ordered alarm grey 3'.

Within minutes, the front page of *News for the Troops* was revised. Across the top of it spread the banner headline 'ATLANTIC WALL BREACHED IN SEVERAL PLACES'. A few hours later it was being rained down on the German positions. It was several hours, too, in advance of any official release of the news.

During the ensuing months Delmer's unit became more deeply engaged than ever in breaking down the moral resistance of the German troops, and the Allied forces penetrated further into the German homeland of the civilian population. Not only did they step up their normal working tactics, but they had to cope also with such extraordinary events as the 20th July attempt on Hitler's life.

Under government instructions, the BBC were forbidden to say anything to encourage the army revolt. They had to make it plain that the Allies still regarded the German officer corps co-responsible with Hitler for the war. Nothing but unconditional surrender would be acceptable, even if the Nazis were totally exterminated by German resistance. This was an incredible decision which I shall never, personally, be able to understand.

Delmer's Soldatensender, however, was on quite a different footing from the BBC and he could impose his own ideas, subject, of course, to the approval of his immediate chiefs, who were very, very unsympathetic. As Delmer has written, the official line threw 'the task of dividing the Germans therefore right back into the laps of the "black" men'; in other words, of him and his fellow black propagandists. This he decided to do, and as an initial step gave instructions that as many 'members of the Wehrmacht, Foreign Office and Administration', as possible, should be involved in the 'peace offensive'.

The star of this campaign was Der Chef. The demise of Gustav Siegfried Eins had been deliberately planned in order that Der Chef might become available to the new radio projects, especially Soldatensender. When Dr Robert Ley, the coarse, uncouth Nazi leader, made an attack on the officer corps, Der Chef made a strong, typical attack on him. Ley, he said, had made himself rich at the expense of the German taxpayer. He owned a number of country and town houses – the whereabouts of which were given – but he had not opened a single one to evacuees from the bombed cities. Young Count Stauffenberg, however, who had led the revolt against Hitler had 'been out at the Front fighting the war which has made this

Ley a multi-millionaire'. This Der Chef followed with many more talks in a similar vein.

Only one of the men involved in the 20th July plot managed to escape abroad and ultimately reached England. He was Otto John, who in the 1950s suddenly disappeared behind the Iron Curtain. The West German Government declared he had defected and had handed his intelligence secrets to the Communists. When John just as suddenly reappeared some years later, he was arrested, tried and sentenced. He has always claimed that he did not defect, but was kidnapped. Since his release he has fought a constant, but up to now vain, struggle to clear his name.

When John arrived in England in 1944, Delmer was asked if he would like to have him in his unit. Delmer realised that such a man, if his bona fides were satisfactory, could be invaluable to him, and when, after an interview, he decided that John was genuinely anti-Hitler, he invited him to work with him. John agreed eagerly, and it was as a result of what the German told him about Himmler's attempts to contact German Resistance that Delmer launched another of his campaigns, which he called 'Himmler for President'.

Apparently in August 1943 Himmler had been much impressed by the views expressed to him by Johannes Popitz, a veteran German Conservative politician, who stressed the urgent need for peace to be made with the West, which he believed to be possible, thus leaving Germany free to concentrate on annihilating the Russians. From this time on, Himmler became quietly obsessed by the idea, and he sent his personal lawyer Dr Langbehn to Switzerland to put out feelers, on similar terms that he asked Count Bernadotte to approach the Allies in April 1945.

Langbehn's mission became known to Hitler, and to save himself Himmler arrested the lawyer when he returned from Berne.

Himmler's plan was to depose Hitler and the other Nazi leaders, which, with his various security forces, he was capable of doing, and to present himself to the Allies as the new humane and reasonable leader. In return for peace in the West, he would ask for Allied support against the Russians.

Using this as the basis for his campaign, Delmer had considerable fun in trying to present Himmler to the Germans as 'the people's friend'. Soldatensender announced that Himmler himself was conducting such a campaign, and one item broadcast stated, 'The personal photo-reporter attached to the Reichsführer SS, SS Sturmbannführer Paul Kurbjuhn, after a careful study of the physiognomy of Heinrich Himmler, has come to the conclusion that the left side of the Reichsführer's face has a kindlier expression than his right profile which gives a more masculine and martial impression. SS Sturmbannführer Kurbjuhn has accordingly decreed that for internal service use in the SS pictures are to be issued showing predominantly the right side of the Reichsführer's face while the left side is to be preferred for shots showing the Reichsführer SS in friendly conversation with folkcomrades or with children'.

Another item in the campaign was the counterfeiting of copies of the German soldier's oath of loyalty to the Führer, but with Himmler's name substituted for Hitler's. Copies of these were distributed in Germany by SOE agents, and a photo-copy appeared in *News for the Troops*.

Delmer was able to procure copies of a morale-boosting propaganda sheet which Himmler was distributing to the soldiers on the Western Front. A feature of these sheets was a correspondence column run by someone who called himself Scorpion. Scorpion invited the troops to send him questions about any matter on which they felt uncertain, and he would answer them with the plain unvarnished truth.

Delmer had a number of these sheets forged, concentrating chiefly on the Scorpion feature, for which Der Chef was responsible. The Der Chef Scorpion's objective was naturally to depress the German soldier instead of raising his morale. Some of Der Chef's questions could have been put by soldiers, and the answers he gave were those which the real Scorpion would have given; but among the phoney questions was this one: 'May the Führer capitulate?' To this Der Chef replied, 'No! If the Führer shows the slightest sign of wanting to give in, then in accordance with the order of the Reichsführer SS of 18th October 1944, the command must be taken over by the next highest Führer who is willing to carry on the fight. The Reichsführer SS knew what he was doing when he issued that order'.

A large batch of the forged sheets carrying this Scorpion question and answer were dropped over the German lines – Himmler delivered his genuine ones in this way – in mid-November 1944. Unfortunately some of them fell into the hands of American intelligence who, believing them to be genuine, found Der Chef's reply highly significant, and had the document rushed to the headquarters of General Edwin L Sibert, who was commanding that sector of the front. Sibert was equally impressed and requested the Operational command to allow him to launch an attack on his sector in view of the demoralised state of the enemy troops opposite.

By a happy chance, Donald McLachlan of PWD, whose original idea the false Scorpion had been, was attending the conference at which the leaflet was discussed by Sibert's intelligence staff. McLachlan tried to intervene to say that the leaflet was a forgery, but was interrupted by Sibert who said he was forwarding it to General Omar Bradley. It was not until the conference ended that McLachlan was able to take Sibert on one side and explain, luckily in time to stop the leaflet from reaching Bradley. Sibert's immediate reaction was anger, but he quickly appreciated the real significance of the trick and took it in good part.

With the advent of 1945 and the failure of Hitler's Ardennes offensive, without slackening the impetus of the established psychological warfare programme, Delmer's unit was able to give its attention to a number of side-lines, all of them of considerable merit. Among them was the issue of drastic evacuation orders to the German civilian population in the name of the Authorities.

Delmer was by this time able to command the services of a very powerful transmitter, which was capable of taking over a German wave-length in half a second. When the RAF raided Germany, the German transmitters in the area of the raid closed down, so that our pilots could not use them as a homing device.

It was over this transmitter that Delmer's first evacuation orders were broadcast. Having found out in advance that the RAF were scheduled to raid Cologne, he prepared his orders. These declared that enemy armour was approaching the city and that women and children must leave their homes at once, 'this very night, taking only fifteen kilograms of baggage with them. The men must stay behind with the

Home Guard to defend the villages and the city'. The women and children were to take handcarts, perambulators, bicycles and anything else on wheels that was available. They were told where to cross the Rhine, and assembly points on the other side were described. There they would find trains waiting to take them to evacuation centres in Bavaria.

The Germans made considerable use of broadcasting at this time for issuing all kinds of instructions to the civilian population. The Cologne announcers used for this were a man and a woman, and Delmer had in his unit a man and a woman whose voices closely resembled those of the Cologne couple.

The plan worked perfectly. The object was to clog the German roads with refugees who would impede the activities of the Wehrmacht. And this was what happened.

Not until Hitler had put an end to his life in his Berlin *bunker* did the PWD slacken its efforts. But with the ceremony on Luneberg Heath their task was done. It is difficult to assess the value of Delmer's stratagems. When the war effort is taken as a whole, they represented but a tiny fraction; but there can be little doubt they made a supremely worthwhile contribution to victory.

# 5 : Rumour

No ONE KNEW quite how it started, but the rumour was passed on in every pub, club and restaurant in Great Britain. It had never happened to the raconteur, but went something like this: 'I say, a friend of mine at the office met a chap who has just come back from a holiday in Germany and the army were on manœuvres. In a lane they accidentally "bumped" into a German tank and it literally fell to pieces – it was an ordinary car chassis covered with plywood. Honestly, who does Hitler think he's bluffing!'

This rumour grew stronger and stronger throughout 1937 and 1938 and there is no doubt that it lulled hundreds of thousands in Britain and on the Continent into a sense of false security. It had its origins in Goebbels's Ministry of Propaganda and Enlightenment, as did two other rumours – that the Wehrmacht's fuel resources were sufficient for only one month's fighting; and that German food supplies would permit only a starvation-level ration; what the tourists saw and ate was a show put on specially for them.

They were clever rumours, and it was doubly unfortunate that at the time that they were gathering momentum, Stanley Baldwin had declared in the House of Commons that Britain had 'a greater air force than any other country within striking distance of our shores'. This statement by the Prime Minister fooled the people of Great Britain – though not the German authorities – and, added to Goebbels's two efforts, had the further effect of damping down any apprehensiveness that might have stimulated a nation-wide demand that something should be done to repair Britain's defences.

The potential of the rumour was appreciated by the psychological warfare experts, who lost little time in making it a weapon in their subsequently varied armoury, though when it was first employed it was one of the few really psychological weapons available. This was in the summer of 1940, after Dunkirk and the fall of France, when England not only stood alone to face Hitler, but did so with an army mostly equipped with broomsticks, bill-hooks and scythes!

It was believed in high places that Hitler would surely attempt to follow up his tremendous successes in western Europe by invading England before she had had time to reorganise and re-equip her forces. We know now that this was, indeed, his intention, and that he was only dissuaded from carrying it out when the RAF proved to him that Goering's boasts about the fighting strength and skill of his Luftwaffe had been even more empty than Baldwin's about the RAF four years earlier. Nevertheless, he had a fleet of invasion barges assembled in the Channel ports, ready to launch *Operation Sea Lion*, as he called it, as soon as the British had been deprived of their aircover, and weather and tides were favourable. We were really in a desperate plight no matter how we might have rallied to Churchill's stentorian call, 'We shall fight on the beaches, we shall fight on the landing-grounds, we shall fight in the fields and in the streets, we shall fight in the hills; we shall never surrender'. If the crunch had come we should have been hard put to it to put up an effective resistance. Every unorthodox weapon, every unorthodox means we possessed of making the enemy pause, we could not afford to overlook. One of these weapons was a rumour that we had discovered how to set fire to the sea, which, though it was nine-tenths rumour, was one-tenth reality.

The pause after the fall of France was a welcome breathing space for the German troops. But they had not been stretched to the limits, and they recovered quickly; probably too quickly for the comfort of their commanders. For soon the comparatively easy and dull existence of standing guard on the Channel coasts, after the exciting dash through France, began to engender in them a restlessness, which if it were not rapidly appeased might engulf them in a fatal boredom. That this did not happen was due to two complementary factors – that presently they would be crossing the narrow seas and landing among the orchards and hop-gardens of Kent, and the fear that when they attempted this invasion the British would try to hold them off by setting fire to the sea.

This belief was conceived one early afternoon in late September when a young German officer on guard on the coast caught the acrid smell of smoke wafting in from the sea. As he watched, he caught sight of thick, black clouds billowing up into the sky, increasing in density and height as each minute passed. By the time he had focused his binoculars, fog was settling over the Channel, and with the aid of his glasses he could discern not only smoke, but a wall of flame a hundred feet high and many yards wide, stretching along the Kent coast. Though he could not believe it, it looked as though the sea was on fire.

Having alerted his superiors, and they theirs, Luftwaffe aircraft were detailed to try to discover

93

what the British were up to. The pilots found this extremely difficult to carry out, for as the flames died down, and the aircraft descended for a closer look, suddenly the tongues of fire would shoot up again, as though controlled.

At the same time that this was happening on the south coast, a similar demonstration was intriguing the crews of German E-boats as they sheltered behind the buoys off the coast of East Anglia, waiting for coastal convoys of merchantmen to pass by. Like the Luftwaffe airmen, the E-boat sailors could make neither head nor tail of what the British were doing if they were not setting fire to the sea.

As these somewhat alarming reports came in, and the General Staff in France had to confess themselves as bewildered as their scouts, it was decided to inform OKW (High Command) headquarters in Berlin immediately, who brought the matter to the attention of the Führer. Hitler had always held the view that fire was the most effective weapon whereby to create terror, chaos and death. He had instructed Goering to give the same priority to the production of the incendiary as to the explosive bomb, and it was he who had provided the title of the first German war propaganda film *Baptism of Fire* – the account of the Polish campaign.

Winston Churchill was directly responsible for these experiments with fire. Checking our stocks of ammunition for meeting the invasion, should it come, the figures for Sten-gun and rifle were pathetically small. In his dramatic way, he reduced the problem to starkly practical proportions – there would be but one bullet for each 2000 German soldiers even if they landed only in moderate strength.

That evening a guest for dinner was Brendan

94

Bracken, the peacetime Chairman of the *Financial News*, the Prime Minister's Parliamentary Private secretary in 1940. It was obvious to Bracken that Churchill was preoccupied and troubled. 'He seemed to be wrestling with a problem,' he wrote later, 'to which he could not find an answer – he was unlike his usual self; he was neither angry nor calm, he seemed to be searching through his mind as he always did, but this time it was different. Suddenly he thumped the table and said "Burning oil! That's what they used – burning oil!" '

The Minister of Fuel, the Chief of the Imperial General Staff, and the liaison officer between the War Cabinet and Chiefs of Staff (General Ismay) were alerted for an important meeting at noon next day. That done, a benign but slightly mysterious Prime Minister retired to bed.

The meeting at noon was over within the hour. As the Minister and Generals were returning to their respective offices, Churchill began to dictate to a secretary one of his famous minutes headed *Action This Day*. He informed all concerned that if 'we cannot blast them (the Germans), we will burn them'.

That same afternoon saw the creation of a new unit and, in two or three rooms in Millbank, Brigadier Sir Donald Banks set up his Petroleum Warfare Department. Around him he gathered technical men from all the major oil companies and the Government Fuel Research Station; he hi-jacked Dr F H Graven from his work as professor of chemical engineering; and he requisitioned a group of Royal Engineers.

The speed with which the department was set up is illustrated by what happened to Captain Eric Hardiman who, after just over a year in the Army, was snatched from his unit and within twenty-four hours

95

was reporting as a civilian to PWD. Eric Hrrdiman, who was a research chemist with Standard Oil, has said, 'It was fantastic. Completely out of the blue, I was out of uniform, put on the reserve and "relegated to unemployment" all in one day. It was a shock, not only because it happened, but that the Army could work so fast'.

To begin with, PWD devised a decoy fire system around oil refineries and petroleum terminals. These dummy-tank fire units consisted of circular trenches about one foot in diameter, lined with clay and containing a layer of breeze and clinker into which oil could be fed. The oil could be ignited by a series of electrically operated fireworks made of black powder and magnesium-alloy turnings scrounged from aircraft factories. The complete device was controlled from a suitably sandbagged shelter where the operator would wait until sufficient air activity was centred around the target area, when he would press a button, and up would go the dummy tanks. Greater realism was obtained later in the way of sudden surges of extra flames by the expedient of petrol-filled lavatory cisterns operated by remote-controlled chains.

There must have been many spurious reports of 'large fires started in oil-refining targets' given by Luftwaffe pilots to their intelligence officers when PWD went into action.

Within weeks a method of 'setting the sea on fire' had been devised. Those residents in the restricted areas of Kent and East Anglia who were still allowed the use of their homes were puzzled by the activities of workmen with picks and shovels busily digging in the hedgerows and planting large tanks every hundred yards. What intrigued them most about the operation was the great care the workmen took in covering the tanks after they had been planted, and the frequent inspections that were carried out when the work, which seemed to stretch for mile after mile, was completed. How was it, they wondered, that in wartime labour could be used to erect pedestrian handrails along paths and pavements in the most unlikely and seemingly useless places?

The truth lay on Sir Donald Banks's desk in Millbank. Each of the tanks contained forty gallons of oil. They were linked together electrically and each had an explosive charge attached to it. In the event of invasion each would be capable of setting one hundred yards of road on fire to a height of ten feet. They were operated remotely, in units of four, thus making it possible for them to be put into action with considerable flexibility.

Tests had proved that no man or machine would be able to live in the inferno they would create. As for the handrails, their function was but a camouflage, for they were perforated tubes and could be fed from hidden oil supplies; and when in action could throw an unbroken flame from both sides of the road. They, too, were operated from remote points to ensure maximum devastation and death.

The work was followed with the keenest interest by the Prime Minister who made frequent tours of inspection, and bombarded PWD with an incessant stream of minutes beginning 'Pray inform me'. The mildness of the tone of these minutes differed from the tone of the voice on the telephone if the answer was not on his desk within the hour.

When this shore barrage had been completed, work was begun on PWD's *pièce de résistance*. Pipe-lines were laid out to sea over a wide area of the coast and fed from a bomb-proof pumping-station five miles inland, with electrically controlled ignition on the surface of the water. It was a simple operation, but its results could be so terrifying that the very thought of using it appalled even the inventors. The radiant heat alone could scorch for miles, and it could be operated continuously and controlled as easily as an oil-fired domestic central-heating installation.

Simple it may have been, but one thing was certain – not even a warship, let alone a landing barge, would be able to survive within half-a-mile of this impenetrable barrier of fire, the evidence of which the soldiers on the Calais cliffs, the pilots in their aircraft and the sailors in their E-boats saw on that sunny September afternoon. Churchill, watching the exhibition, chuckled, 'Herr Hitler may not have a beard like Philip of Spain, but this will certainly singe his moustache'.

With this weapon PWD firmly established itself. Not content to rest on their laurels, Sir Donald Banks and his team carried out a ceaseless stream of experiments into ways and means of using burning oil as a weapon. One such experiment was carried out by Captain Hardiman from Waterloo Bridge.

Hardiman was trying to discover the potential of a small bomb that would explode on impact with water and eject blazing gelignite on to floating oil, for use in enemy harbours after aerial attack. The Thames River Police volunteered to recover the spent bombs from the water for expert examination. The experiment was not repeated – at least not in the Thames, nor with the co-operation of the River Police. For the bombs were so effective that they set fire to Waterloo Bridge pier.

Not long after this, Psychological Warfare forwarded to Millbank a German leaflet sent to it by SOE agents in Germany. It informed German fire-watchers that

British incendiary bombs could be rendered harmless by immersion in a bucket of water or by spraying them. PWD immediately set about producing a new type of bomb which exploded with sufficient force to blow up a fair-sized house if it came into contact with an egg-cupful of water.

Before its illustrious career came to a close, PWD created some of the seven wonders of the war – the perfected flamethrower and, in particular, PLUTO, the *Pipe Line Under the Ocean*, which carried oil from Britain under the Channel to supply the Allied forces invading Normandy. These were, of course, tremendous successes; but taken in conjunction with the desperate situation at the time, in my view, 'Setting the sea on fire' was the department's greatest achievement.

PWD cannot, however, take all the glory for the success which the rumour had – for it was a rumour. Though the sea fire-barrage could have been operated for a time, it was too costly in oil to use for more than a few hours. But there was no need for that – just a few brief moments of 'testing' and a well-planted rumour by Psychological Warfare sufficed.

In the bars of Lisbon and Stockholm, Berne and Madrid agents began to whisper – 'The English can set the sea on fire'. Agents of the French Resistance gave it gleeful currency in stage-whispers that could be heard all over France.

Yet for a time it looked to the launchers of the whisper campaign as though it were not going to work. Weeks went by, and there was no indication that the Germans had taken it to heart even if they had heard of it. Then one day the pilot of a damaged aircraft baled out over my former home-village of Charing, in Kent. On being asked, he admitted that

99

all his unit knew about the 'burning sea defences'. From then on evidence came in that the rumour had achieved very wide circulation indeed; so wide, in fact, that the German High Command had heard of it, and had been assured by their scientific experts that it was feasible, if costly. Hitler at once gave orders for experiments to be made in proofing the invasion barges with asbestos.

The first of these experiments, carried out at Fécamp, was a ghastly failure. A barge 'armoured' with asbestos sheeting was filled with troops and sailed through a pool of burning petrol. All in it were burned to death.

The badly charred bodies that were washed up at various points along the French coast gave rise to another rumour. It became widely believed among the German forces in France that an invasion attempt had been made and foiled by the English setting the sea on fire.

Though those who were responsible for the campaign had taken the utmost precautions to keep it from their own people, the rumour was soon in circulation in Britain. People in Dover and Newhaven had actually seen German soldiers being landed, their heads and hands swathed in bandages; hideously charred bodies had been secretly buried among the sand-dunes of Sandwich Bay; vast quantities of anti-burn dressings were collected from hospitals all over England and rushed to the east and south-east coasts. It raised morale here at a time when it was much needed.

# 6 : The Art of Deception

HARD ON THE heels of rumour as a psychological
weapon comes the art of deliberate deception. By this
is meant the deliberate attempt to mislead the enemy
not merely by words but by acts or camouflage or
some concrete means of making him believe that one's
own strength or intentions are other than they actually
are. The first example that comes readily to mind is
the 'removal' of Birnam Woods to Dunsinane in the
legend of Macbeth, when, it will be recalled, Malcolm
and Macduff, in their attack on Macbeth's castle,
had their troops cut down branches from the trees in
Birnam Woods, and each man, holding a branch
which concealed him from view from the castle, crept
slowly forward.

This kind of practical deception is as old as history
itself. Somewhere about the year 203 BC Rome was
at war with Carthage, and in North Africa the
brilliant young Roman general Scipio Africanus was
facing one of Carthaginian Hannibal's strongest allies,
Syphax, King of Numidia. Scipio had decided that if
his own armies were to be reasonably sure of ultimate
victory, Syphax must first be eliminated. He did not
know, however, the exact strength of the Numidians,
nor the disposition of their defences.

With a display of cunning not at all in tune with
the chivalrous conduct of war, Scipio proposed to
Syphax an armistice with the aim of arranging peace

terms, while in fact he intended that his negotiators should gauge the strength of Syphax's army, and note the nature of his defence works. Since skilled soldiers would be required to collect this information, Scipio was faced with a difficulty, for if Syphax saw that the Roman deputation was composed of military men, he would undoubtedly become suspicious. After a good deal of consideration, Scipio eventually solved the problem by the appointment of civilians who had accompanied the Roman armies, and sending with them skilled soldiers disguised as slaves.

That Syphax would be suspicious was fully substantiated by his stipulation that the Roman deputation and their attendants, civilians though they were, should remain within the compound allotted to them and that if they wished to move about the camp at all, they must be accompanied by Numidian officers.

In command of the 'slaves' Scipio had sent his great friend and general, Laelius. Confronted with this restriction on his movements, Laelius instructed the deputation to draw out the discussions as long as possible, so that he might try to devise some way of obtaining the information for which he had come. But as day after day passed, neither opportunity nor plan presented itself, until eventually the head of the delegation said firmly that he could play for time no longer. Laelius begged for twenty-four hours more. If he had not succeeded by then, he would give up.

As he sat among his 'slaves', trying desperately to conjure up some scheme, suddenly one of the horses neighed loudly and reared, possibly under a more than usually vicious attack from a fly. As one of the men ran to the horse to calm it, Laelius was suddenly inspired. Calling his men to him, he told them that they were surreptitiously to provoke the horses to become restless. They were then to appear to be trying to quieten them, but they were in fact to increase the provocation until the horses began to stampede. They would chase after the animals, ineptly attempt to catch them, but all the while edge them nearer and nearer to the Numidian defence works, and, if possible, inside them.

The plan succeeded. The horses, with the 'slaves' in pursuit, entered the defences, and by the time they were caught, not a detail of the Numidian fortifications and the effective strength of their armies were unknown to the Romans. The following day the negotiations were broken off. Shortly afterwards Scipio attacked Syphax, set fire to the defences, and so completely routed the Numidians that they were compelled to withdraw to their own country, where they were still licking their wounds when Scipio and Hannibal met on the battlefield of Zama, and the contest ended with the permanent defeat of Carthage.

A thousand years earlier, the Greeks had deceived the Trojans with their wooden horse, and the withdrawal of their fleet out of sight of the city, so that it looked as if they had sailed away, while Sinon persuaded the relieved citizens to drag the horse inside the walls. Just over a thousand years later than Zama, William the Bastard deceived the Saxons at Hastings into believing that his troops were genuinely retreating, and when Harold's men followed in headlong pursuit suddenly rounded on them.

Nearly a thousand years after Hastings, the British Admiralty for a time slowed down the U-boat attacks on merchant shipping by the use of Q-ships. Q-ships were old merchant ships reprieved from the breaker's yard, made seaworthy, armed with guns camouflaged by screens, and crewed by naval officers and ratings.

Posing as an aged merchantman, a Q-ship would haunt the shipping lanes. When challenged by a U-boat, part of the crew would scramble for the lifeboats, whereupon the U-boat would surface, and because there was a shortage of torpedoes in the German Navy at this time, approach to sink the Q-ship with gunfire. As soon as the German was within effective range of their guns, the members of the Q-ship crew remaining concealed on board would throw down the screens, haul down the Red Ensign and hoist the White, and attack – and sink – the U-boat.

The Royal Navy have always been past-masters at this kind of deception and have used other methods also with great skill. Indeed, they began the Second World War with a trick which rid them of one of their most powerful enemies.

At quarter past six on the morning of 13th December 1939, Commodore Henry Harwood stood on the bridge of the British cruiser *Ajax* aware that Naval intelligence, as so often in the past, had scored yet another bull's-eye. For, in the distance, he could just discern the superstructure of the German pocket-battleship the *Admiral Graf Spee*, appearing above the horizon.

Harwood had followed the *Graf Spee*'s progress in the South Atlantic from the moment she had sunk her first victim, the ss *Clement*, off Pernambuco, on 30th September. With her last signals, the *Clement* had indicated that she had been attacked by a warship and not an armed merchant-cruiser. This important news was the first indication that enemy raiders were at sea; Winston Churchill had at once ordered that a long-planned operation should begin.

From his experience the First Lord knew that the

only way to combat surface-raiders was to have squadrons sweeping the seven seas. Six such squadrons were allocated to the south Atlantic for there, the Germans knew, they would find their richest prizes. One of these squadrons was commanded by Commodore Harwood.

While Harwood and his ships had been patrolling the area allocated to him, in the Admiralty fortress in London the ears of the Royal Navy had been strained to catch the slightest whisper of the whereabouts of the *Graf Spee*. They had not listened in vain, but as they had converted these whispers to courses plotted on charts, they realised that in Captain Langsdorff they had a cunning quarry, well skilled in covering up his tracks.

After the sinking of the *Clement*, Langsdorff had sent four ships to the bottom between the Ascension Islands and St Helena. This was followed by the news that he had raced round the Cape of Good Hope where another sinking was reported off Madagascar. Then there had been silence for a time, and now another ship had been attacked once more off St Helena.

To those who knew about these things, the indications were that the *Graf Spee's* next objective would be shipping in the main lanes from South America. Piecing together the reports sent him by Naval intelligence, Commodore Harwood believed that the enemy battleship was heading for the mouth of the River Plate, and had steamed in that direction himself, with the rest of his squadron – the 8-inch cruiser *Exeter*, and the 6-inch cruiser *Achilles*, and called up the 8-inch cruiser *Cumberland* from the Falkland Islands, where she was refitting.

Harwood had calculated that the *Graf Spee* would

arrive off the Plate on the night of the 12th or the morning of the 13th December; and here she was.

Harwood immediately ordered his ships to stations from which the attack on the battleship could be launched, and then advanced at top speed to meet the German. Apparently, Captain Langsdorff thought that he had to deal with only one light cruiser and two destroyers – a force which he felt he could out-gun – instead of three cruisers; and he, too, increased speed towards the British ships heading for the *Exeter*.

At 6.17 am he opened fire with his superior 11-inch guns, which the *Exeter* immediately returned, scoring hits. At the same time, the *Ajax* and *Achilles* had opened fire with good effect, but presently the *Graf Spee* scored a hit on the *Exeter* which not only knocked out B turret and destroyed all the communications on the bridge, killing all there, but put the cruiser temporarily out of control. Fortunately, Langsdorff was prevented from giving the *Exeter* the *coup de grâce* on account of the telling fire of the other two ships, and this gave the cruiser time to collect herself and bring her rear guns to train on the battleship.

Now realising that the opposition was much stronger than he had believed it to be, he turned away under a smokescreen, with the apparent intention of making for the River Plate. After a gallant attempt to keep up his attack, Captain Bell had to pull the *Exeter* out of the action, as she was burning fiercely amidships and listing heavily. Undeterred by this the *Ajax* and *Achilles*, though outmatched, continued the chase. The *Graf Spee* brought all her heavy guns to bear on them, and by 7.25 had knocked out the two after-turrets of the *Ajax* and seriously damaged the *Achilles*. As his ammunition was now running low, Harwood decided to break off the engagement until after dark.

For the rest of the day the *Graf Spee* kept course for Montevideo, the British ships hanging at her heels, and shortly after midnight she entered the Uruguayan harbour, where she landed her wounded and began to repair her damage. Harwood stationed his two ships outside in the roads, determined to renew the battle when the German emerged.

This she would have to do sooner or later, for under international law a belligerent ship may only seek refuge in a neutral harbour until she has carried out essential repairs. The Uruguayan authorities calculated that Langsdorff would require twenty-four hours in which to do this, and gave him the ultimatum to be gone within this period. When, however, Langsdorff asked for an extension and was genuinely seen to be unready to put to sea, they allowed him another twenty-four hours, but made it quite clear that he would have to go when these had expired, whether he was ready or not.

Meanwhile, the Admiralty had ordered up other forces in support of the *Exeter* and *Ajax*. But the nearest ships were too far away to arrive in time should Langsdorff decide to make a break for it, and it was at this point that deception was resorted to.

The Admiralty sent to Harwood a signal that the aircraft carrier *Ark Royal* and the battleship *Renown* were joining him and would arrive within a few hours. They knew that Langsdorff would receive this news either through his own interceptors or the German Admiralty, for they sent it in a code which they knew the Germans could break.

Not knowing that the *Ark Royal* and the *Renown* were several hundred miles away, Langsdorff decided to scuttle his ship rather than face defeat at the hands of this vastly superior force.

At 6.15 pm on 17th December, watched by huge crowds ashore, the *Graf Spee* steamed out of Montevideo. At 8.54 the *Ajax's* reconnaissance aircraft reported, '*Graf Spee* has blown herself up'.

On 19th December, Langsdorff, an honourable man, shot himself.

The Royal Air Force and the Army were no less adept at deception, and the great pains with which they executed their plans were made worthwhile by the success that attended them. Counterfeit airfields were laid out, complete with plywood aircraft near to real airfields, and many a German bomb was dropped on the models while the true airfield escaped damage. During the night raids on airfields, fires would be lit or dummy flare-paths illuminated some way from the actual German target to mislead the Luftwaffe pilots and their bomb-layers.

At Alamein, General Montgomery deceived his adversary Rommel by an elaborate deception plan in the classic style. Dummy lorries, counterfeit supply dumps, five miles of dummy railway track, dummy pump-houses and tanks were all included in the great deception. But without doubt the greatest deception of the Second World War was designed and executed to mislead the German High Command as to where the Allies would land in their attempt to liberate Europe.

One day in the late spring of 1944, a month or so before the Allies began their invasion of Normandy, a group of high-ranking officers stood on the tarmac at Gibraltar airport awaiting the arrival of an aircraft bringing a very important military person to the Rock. Presently the aircraft came in sight, landed, taxied across the runway to the waiting group and came to a halt. The doors slid back as the steps were trundled into place, and almost at once there appeared at the top General Montgomery, the victor of Alamein, and at this time Commander-in-Chief Land Forces for the invasion of Europe.

The General paused briefly and gave his characteristic salute. He then ran down the steps and hurried over to the group of officers and said a few words of greeting. This done, he asked loudly if a Major Foley were present.

The Major stepped forward and saluted.

'Good,' remarked the General. 'We'll get along to Government House right away.'

'This way, sir,' said Foley and led Montgomery to the nearest motor-car.

On the short journey to Government House, the General kept up a lively flow of conversation with the Major, telling him that he had had a good flight to Gibraltar, and asking how the Governor, General Sir Ralph Eastwood, was.

'He's very fit, sir,' Foley told him, 'and looking forward to seeing you again.'

'It seems no time at all since we were at Sandhurst together,' Montgomery commented.

Word of the General's arrival on the Rock had quickly spread, and as the car went on its way, troops came running from all directions waving and shouting 'Good old Monty!' though many of them must have wondered what he was doing there, since it was generally thought that the Allied invasion of Europe was to be made from the south coast of Britain into Normandy and Brittany.

As the car turned into the gates of Government House, the General saluted the fair-sized crowd that had gathered there. Waiting to receive him, he could see, was the Governor, while a guard of honour sprang to attention and presented arms.

Montgomery got out of the car, saluted and went forward to greet Sir Ralph Eastwood, as Sir Ralph came towards him, smiling, his hand outstretched.

'Hallo, Monty, it's good to see you again,' the Governor exclaimed.

'How are you, Rusty?' Monty replied. 'You're looking very fit.'

'You, too, Monty. Did you have a good trip?'

'Excellent. Fine weather all the way.'

With the familiarity of friendship, Montgomery took the Governor by the arm and they went into the house. In Sir Ralph's study, the Governor took off his hat and sat down at his desk in dead silence. For a moment or two he just sat and stared at the General, then presently he began to smile. Getting up, he hurried across to him, and shook him warmly by the hand.

'I wouldn't have believed it possible,' he exclaimed. 'You're simply splendid. I can't get over it. You *are* Monty. I've known him for years, but you're so much like him that for a few moments I thought he had changed the plan and decided to come here himself.'

'I'm glad you think I look the part, sir,' Lieutenant M E Clifton James replied with relief.

Thus began the greatest deception of all time.

Lieutenant M E Clifton James had seen service in the First World War, and had been wounded on the Somme. In civilian life he was an actor but on the outbreak of the Second World War he had joined up again and had been posted to the Army Pay Corps at Leicester.

His striking resemblance to General Montgomery had first been brought home to him when, after the victories in North Africa, he had gone onto the stage of a Nottingham theatre to make an announcement and had been enthusiastically received by the audience, who thought he was Montgomery come to address them. Not long afterwards, he was giving a Sunday night performance of *When Knights Were Bold* at the Comedy Theatre in London with an Army theatrical company. After the show a *News Chronicle* photographer had gone to his dressing-room and asked if he might take a photograph of him, as he looked so very like the General. James had agreed, and a day or two later one of the photographs appeared in the newspaper with the caption, 'You're Wrong – It's Lieutenant Clifton James.'

The retribution which James had expected to follow this incident not descending, he forgot his alleged likeness to Montgomery. Then one day in April 1944 he had a telephone call from Colonel David Niven, Assistant Director of Army Kinematograph. Colonel Niven asked him if he would be interested in making some army films, and when he replied that he would be, told him to approach his Commanding Officer and ask for seven days' unofficial attachment to the film unit and go to London.

With some difficulty, James obtained his CO's permission, but before he departed for London he was visited by a Colonel Lester. They had lunch together, and chatted about this and that. Only after Lester had gone did James realise that they had not said a single word about films.

James had been instructed to report to an address in Curzon Street, in London, and there he was met by Colonel Niven, who, after a minute or two of affable chat, handed him over once more to Colonel Lester. Lester told him bluntly, 'I'm afraid I've got rather a shock for you. You aren't going to make any films'.

Someone had suggested that as General Montgomery could be expected to command our invasion forces, if he were to appear in a theatre of war far removed from northern France, the Germans might be led to believe that the invasion was going to take place somewhere in the Mediterranean, probably in southern France, or on the Greek peninsula. Any trick that could help to deceive the Germans and persuade them to dissipate their strength by assembling troops in the wrong area was well worth trying. The trouble was, of course, that with D-Day only a few weeks away, Montgomery could not spare the time from the planning board, and so a double would have to be found to take his place on the proposed tour of inspection.

The substitute would not only have to be Monty's double in looks, but someone who would be able to imitate his voice and reproduce his mannerisms – in fact, an actor of considerable ability, since he would have to succeed in deceiving people who knew Monty at close quarters. Hollywood and the acting fraternity in Great Britain were combed, but no one could be found who looked sufficiently like the General. The plan was about to be abandoned when Lieutenant Clifton James's photograph appeared in the *News Chronicle* and was brought to the notice of those in the Deception Department allocated to organise the scheme. James fitted the part perfectly as far as looks were concerned, and if he proved to have an histrionic ability which would make it possible for him to play the part in other respects, the Greatest Deception would be well on the road to success.

For some reason, probably because of their familiarity with nefarious conspiracies, MI5, the counter-espionage section of Military Intelligence, were charged with organising the plan, and the three men detailed to mount the operation were Colonel Lester, a professional counter-espionage agent, Captain Stephen Watts, a well-known dramatic critic, and Lieutenant Jack Hervey. All this Colonel Lester now explained to James, adding that if the plan succeeded it would undoubtedly save the lives of many thousands of men.

James had some misgivings about his ability to play the part to the degree of perfection that the plan, by its very nature, demanded, but he agreed, nevertheless, to make an attempt. After several days of conferences at the War Office, he was sent to a large country house – transformed into an I Corps sergeant – as a member of GHQ Staff, with orders to shadow the General wherever he went and to watch him closely to discover his gestures and mannerisms. The first day they went to Portsmouth to watch a dress-rehearsal for D-Day. Returned from this outing, James was convinced that he would never be able to impersonate Monty so well that he would be taken for him, but those in charge of him always had a word of encouragement for him, and gradually his confidence began to assert itself.

Shortly after the Portsmouth visit he was ordered to Scotland to join the General, who was taking a few days' rest and relaxation with half-a-dozen or so members of his personal staff at Dalwhinnie. There he was able to study Montgomery at close quarters.

In his book, *I Was Monty's Double*,[1] James has said, 'He smiled and joked with his staff, took a keen

[1] Rider and Company: London, 1954. I have drawn upon this book for my account here.

interest in the details of each day's excursion even to the extent of having good-natured arguments about how to keep the food fresh and the tea or coffee piping hot. At meals he never monopolised the conversation. He was just a genial master on an outing with some of his boys. . . . The war seemed to be far away. I don't remember hearing him refer to it once. As to his energy, it was astounding . . . the more I studied him, the harder I found it to believe that this dapper, soft-spoken man was to lead our great armies into Hitler's European fortress. There he would stand, smiling at some remark of his youngest officer, as if the great battle before him had already been won.'

On this visit to Scotland, James devoted the whole of his time to studying the General, and also had a personal interview with him. As he said good night at the close of this meeting, Monty said to him, 'You have a great responsibility, you know. Do you feel confident?' James hesitated before replying, and while he did so, Monty said, 'I'm sure everything will be all right. Don't worry about it!' James comments, 'In that moment not only did my qualms vanish but I saw how Monty had only to tell an army that it could do the impossible and it just went and did it'.

After a trip to Devon in a small aircraft to test his reactions to flying – Monty was a good flyer – and a further series of conferences, a dress-rehearsal was held. Now, for the first time, James was told that he was not going to impersonate Montgomery in England while the General went to North Africa, as he had originally been informed, but that he was going to visit North Africa.

The first stage of the journey would end in Gibraltar, where he would stay for a few hours before flying on – to Algiers and Tunis. This stop in Gibraltar had been deliberately planned. In fact, it was one of the most important parts of the whole scheme, for it was known that there were a number of identified German spies on the Rock who would certainly pass on to Berlin the news of Montgomery's arrival in Gibraltar. It was these spies who were James's most important audience. It was these, above all, that he had to deceive, though his deception of others was of almost equal importance since a leak of the impersonation would defeat its ends.

At the dress-rehearsal, James was taken through the scenes which were to be enacted on his arrival in and departure from Gibraltar. When that stage had been successfully completed, he would be coached for the next stage.

By this time James was reaching a state of perfection in his role. Except for Montgomery himself, no one could have impersonated the General better. He still had crises of confidence every now and again, but these were usually dissipated quickly by his coaches. One strange thing did puzzle him and slightly worry him, however. Normally, he explains, an actor only assumes his role on the stage. When he returns to his dressing-room after the final curtain he sheds the character and becomes himself until the next performance. James had discovered that he had so absorbed himself in his role that he was acting it all the time. This was excellent, of course, while the performance lasted; what worried James was the thought that he might never be able to reassume his own personality when the charade was over. He mentioned this fear to his coaches, but they brushed it aside – he would soon re-adapt, they said.

At last the time came for the Greatest Deception to begin in earnest. Colonel Lester appeared for the last time with his reassurances. Provided James did not worry, the Colonel said, he would be absolutely all right.

'You won't be alone,' he added. 'The Brigadier will always be there to help you. But if you do get stuck, just play it off the cuff. Now about money . . . . '

This was the first time the financial aspect of the operation had been mentioned, and what Colonel Lester had to say revealed a lack of imagination in the Treasury difficult to credit.

'You know, don't you,' the Colonel went on, 'that this job is simply part of your duties as a soldier? It was suggested to the War Cabinet that you should be paid danger money.'

'Danger money, sir?'

'Oh yes, you'll be in danger all right. But the Treasury said no. You couldn't draw extra pay for carrying out your duties. However, General Montgomery got to hear of this and he took a strong line about it. He said, "If James is good enough to wear my uniform he's good enough to draw my pay." What pay does he get?'

'I've no idea,' James told him. For once the Colonel's habitual sang-froid was breached, revealing that at this final moment he was human after all.

'Damn it, man!' he exploded. 'You ought to know. You're in the Pay Corps, aren't you?'

'I've never had to deal with a General's account,' James told him.

With a final word of farewell and good wishes, Lester left him. He picked up his hold-all and went into the next room where his two aides, Brigadier Heywood and Captain Moore, were waiting.

'I'm certain you'll be a big success,' the Brigadier said. 'I'll see you at the airport, sir.'

In the street, three large official cars were standing, the leading one flying General Montgomery's personal pennant. A crowd had gathered, and as the cars drew away they cheered.

Somehow, word that Monty was passing had spread, and all the way to the airport groups of people had gathered to wave and cheer. James answered with the famous Monty grin and characteristic salute. At the airfield a number of high-ranking naval and military officers were waiting on the tarmac to see him off. This was his first great test.

The senior officer called the party to attention and saluted. James returned the salute and walked slowly down the line. Nearer the aircraft, the crew was standing. He went over to the captain, and addressing him by name, asked him if he thought the trip would be a good one. The captain smiled and said that the weather reports were good. After inspecting the crew, James mounted the steps to the aircraft, turned for a final salute, and went inside. The success of Act I, scene i, augured well for the play as a whole.

The flight to Gibraltar was not uneventful. Due to an error in fuelling the aircraft, after the point of no return, the captain discovered that there was barely enough petrol to get them to the Rock. In fact, he was of the opinion that they would not be able to reach Gibraltar. Faced by this extraordinary dilemma, the Brigadier decided that if they had to make a forced landing it would be in the sea, and not in Spain, though this would mean certain death for them all. However, in the event, the aircraft did reach the Rock – with petrol for a couple of minutes' flying time in the tanks.

The arrival in Gibraltar, as I have already re-counted, passed off with complete success.

When he had recovered from his surprise at James's

striking resemblance to Monty, the Governor told him that he was now to go to his room and rest. A man who had been Monty's batman for several years, and was attached to Government House, had asked for the privilege of serving him breakfast, and this had been granted. This meeting would be James's stiffest test so far, and in the event he funked it. When the man brought porridge and coffee to his room, James kept his back to him, pretending to be absorbed in some papers.

The arrangement had been that James was to stay in his room until the Governor's ADC, Major Foley, fetched him. Half-an-hour passed and when there was no sign of Foley, he began to grow restless, wondering if anything had gone wrong.

In his nervous pacing about the room, James went to the window. In the square below were one or two taxis and a few loiterers, but a movement on a roof opposite caught his attention, and looking up, he saw a man in a beret holding something that looked like a rifle pointing straight at him. He knew now what Colonel Lester had meant by saying that he would be in danger.

Wondering what to do, for he thought that if he moved he might draw the man's fire, he continued to stare out of the window, and presently he realised that the thing the man was holding was not a rifle but a telescope, which he had trained on the interior of the room. At that moment Foley entered the room full of apologies, and asked him to return to the study.

There Sir Ralph told him that in a few minutes he was going to take him for a walk in the garden at the back of the house. Alterations were being carried out to the left wing of the house, and some scaffolding had been erected. One of the men engaged on the work, the Governor remarked almost casually, was a known enemy agent.

James told him about the man with the telescope who had been spying on him.

'That will be he,' Sir Ralph said. 'It's very obliging of him, because that's what we want. He'll have been making sure you are the General. Now, while we are in the garden two prominent Spaniards – they are supposed to be financiers – are going to call on Lady Eastwood to look at some ancient Moroccan carpets we have. As they pass through the gardens on the way to the house I will introduce you to them.'

There was a stone frieze in the garden, the Governor went on. When he made some remark about it, it would signify that the two men were coming through the garden gates. He explained that the timing of the encounter was very important. To the enemy it had to appear to be a rare coincidence. After a trip of 3000 miles General Montgomery had decided to take a turn in the gardens at the precise moment that two prominent Spaniards called at Government House, and the meeting of the three was purely fortuitous.

James and the Governor went out into the garden, and chatted as they walked. James saw the agent who had been on the roof, but who was now without his telescope, eyeing him intently. Presently the Governor asked, 'Do you remember this frieze?'

At that moment two men came into the garden and began to walk towards them. James at once began to talk loudly about the War Cabinet and Plan 303. Sir Ralph put a hand on his arm as if to warn him, and he broke off abruptly.

The two Spaniards came up, and the Governor introduced James to them. James was polite but aloof, after he had greeted them. He noticed that while one talked animatedly to Sir Ralph, the other looked at him with fierce concentration.

After a few moments' conversation, James said, beginning to turn away, 'Well, I only hope that the weather holds. I have a lot more flying in front of me.'

The Spaniards took their leave, and went on to the house. Later Sir Ralph told him that the men were, in fact, the most important Nazi agents in Spain, and MI5 hoped that this meeting, which had been deliberately planned, would play a major part in deceiving the Germans into believing that General Montgomery was visiting North Africa.

The Governor was extremely pleased with the way the encounter had passed off. He was quite convinced that within a few hours all the world – including Berlin – would know that Monty had visited the Rock.

He then explained to James the next stage of the operation. He was to go on to Algiers in an hour's time. At the airport, whither Sir Ralph would accompany him, he was to draw the Governor aside, and stroll up and down with him under the windows of the canteen, telling him, as they walked, that the War Cabinet had agreed that the African coast was ideal for launching an invasion, and talking about the codes which were to be used, and various other plans. This was for the benefit of a certain Norwegian who worked in the canteen and was known to be a Nazi agent also.

All went well with the departure scene, and in the aircraft Brigadier Heywood congratulated him on what he described as 'a huge success'. After he had rested for a time, the Brigadier explained to him what was to happen next.

Rumours had been carefully put into circulation in Algeria and Tunisia that Monty was coming to North

Africa to organise an Anglo-American force that was to invade southern France and join up with the French Resistance. It was now his task to convince the enemy agents in Algiers that the rumours were true.

On leaving the aircraft at Algiers airport, James inspected British and American guards of honour, after having been greeted by members of General Wilson's staff – General Wilson commanded British troops in North Africa – and was then taken in a huge American motor-car, and, accompanied by a numerous motor-cycle escort, was rushed to Wilson's headquarters. If an attempt were to be made to assassinate Monty, the experts believed it would be made on the journey from the airport to the city, and the Americans were taking no chances.

'The next few days passed in a sort of recurring dream,' James has written. 'Landings, official receptions, guards of honour, bogus talks on high strategy; crowds of civilian spectators, no doubt with enemy agents among them; the streets lined with cheering troops. "Good old Monty!" I saluted and waved. Then back to the airport for the next lap of this curious journey.'

At one place Brigadier Heywood introduced him to a French woman, known to be an enemy agent. The woman's husband had worked in the Resistance and had been captured by the Gestapo, who had informed her that if she wished to see him alive again, she must spy for them. General Montgomery did not approve of women being in the actual war zone, and though James greeted the woman politely enough, there was a curtness in his voice which, he hoped, would reflect the General's dislike.

He exchanged a few words with the woman, but as they chatted suddenly her nerve snapped, and sobbing hysterically she began to denounce him as the high priest of war. Embarrassed, James turned abruptly away, while Brigadier Heywood led her to a motor-car.

At the end of a week James returned to General Wilson's headquarters, his mission completed. 'I drove up to headquarters as Monty, in a blaze of glory, but the moment I passed through the door the glory had gone for ever.'

Now wearing the uniform of a Pay Corps lieutenant, he was taken by a staff colonel out of the house by the back door to a nearby villa.[1] What happened thereafter was bizarre in the extreme.

A day or two later James was smuggled to Cairo. There he lay low for some weeks, and eventually he was put on an ancient rickety Dakota and flown back to England, via Gibraltar. The stop in Gibraltar also seems to me to have been an unnecessary risk. The enemy agents were doubtless still there – in fact, James saw one of them – and James was not instructed to disguise his striking likeness to Monty. Seeing a man who closely resembled the General in a spot where only a week or two previously the General had been

[1] This seems a most extraordinary ending to such a mission. Scores of troops had seen Monty enter Wilson's HQ. None saw him leave. In fact, within minutes he had vanished even from the view of the indoors staff, whose curiosity must have been roused by the sudden evaporation into thin air of the best-known of all British Generals. There must have been discussions about it, and news of the General's vanishing trick could easily have come to the knowledge of enemy agents. Yet, until the invasion of Normandy took place, it was absolutely essential that enemy suspicions about the object of the exercise should not be roused in the slightest degree. If they had the faintest idea that the General their agents had seen in Gibraltar and North Africa was an impersonator, all James's efforts had been in vain. This seems to me a fantastic flaw in an otherwise magnificent scheme.

could have raised doubts which might have affected the whole issue.

The aircraft had to make a forced landing in southwest England, and it was only after several brushes with various Service petty bureaucrats that James at last reached London. Though he was under a vow not to breathe a word of what he had been doing to anyone, no attempt had been made to inform his CO in the Pay Corps at Leicester that he had been engaged on highly secret work. Somewhat naturally the CO was incensed when James suddenly reappeared in his unit, and would have put him on a charge as a deserter if James had not broken his vow.

It is now history that the Greatest Deception was a success. The German leaders were confused about the Allies' true intentions, and Hitler insisted on keeping several divisions in the south of France, even when Rommel was calling for them for the defence of the north. The invasion of Normandy was, in consequence, more easily accomplished than it might otherwise have been, and there can be no doubt that many hundreds of Englishmen and Americans owe their lives to Lieutenant M E Clifton James, the great impostor.

# 7 : V for Victory

THE MAIN AIMS of psychological warfare were to confuse, depress and make nervous both enemy troops
and civilians. If the morale of oneself and one's allies
is raised at the same time, the effect of the campaign
is doubled.

One of the most effective of all PWE's campaigns
was originated by two brilliant men, Victor de
Laveleye, a former member of the Belgian Government, the other, Douglas Ritchie of the BBC's
European news service. Simple in concept, in operation it was to prove one of the most highly successful
operations ever mooted by PWE.

Actually, the basic idea was sparked off by an unknown Belgian who, one evening as our bombers
throbbed their way over his country towards Germany,
scribbled in chalk on a house shutters the letters RAF.
Within two or three weeks hundreds of thousands of
'RAFs' appeared in many likely and many more
unlikely places all over Belgium. The Germans, enraged by the taunting reminder of Goering's announcement at the beginning of the war that no enemy
aircraft would ever be able to penetrate German
sky-space, were helpless to stop it. Soldiers, detailed
to wash away the chalked symbol of Belgian defiance
and courage, were surrounded by crowds of laughing,
jeering men, women and children. As fast as one set
of letters was removed, a score of new ones cropped

up. To attempt to delete them was a sisyphean task, which could never be accomplished.

The idea had spread like wildfire, and in February 1941 the authors of a routine intelligence report made a brief mention of it. Laveleye, in charge of the BBC's Belgian News Service, saw the report, and suddenly the brief item set off a train of thought. Striking a pencil through RAF, he wrote in their place a large V. In English, French and Flemish V is the initial letter of the word meaning Victory. It was far more simple to inscribe than RAF; a downward and upward flick of the hand holding chalk or paintbrush, and there it was.

In his next broadcast to Belgium, Laveleye remarked that he had heard about the RAF campaign, and told his listeners what a good idea it was. He went on to suggest, however, that the better symbol would be the letter V, and explained why. His suggestion caught on at once, and within a couple of weeks he was informed that Belgium was literally inundated by a sea of Vs.

Naturally, others came to hear of what was happening in Belgium, and those who were in a position to do so urged the people of the occupied countries to imitate the Belgians. Soon all Europe was covered in Vs, and the irritated Germans were compelled to resurrect the archaic German word for victory – *Viktoria* – and encourage their own soldiers to chalk up a V now and again, in an attempt to counteract the effect on morale that the campaign was having.

Organised resistance in the occupied countries was not a spontaneous affair. Practically every country could boast one or two outstanding acts of defiance or resistance, but such acts by individuals, except for boosting the morale of a small circle who knew about them, were ineffectual. To be effective there had to be organisation, and, though SOE was progressively infiltrating all the occupied countries, the task of co-ordinating and bringing together the resistant spirits and setting them a programme of activity that made the risks taken and the results achieved worthwhile was more than one body could cope with. Eventually SOE's major role was transmuted into that of adviser and supplier of arms, in which role it excelled. On the other hand, politics seeped into resistance. Believing always in victory, the various political factions, looking forward to the upheaval that peace must bring, became intent on laying up merit for themselves.

This, however, did not begin to happen anywhere for the first two years after the overrunning of their countries. It took this time for the majority of the people to recover from the shock and spiritual numbness which occupation induces. Resistance took the form of a slow awakening, but always there were a few more sturdy individuals who, by their actions, kept, so to speak, the ideal of resistance from ever becoming completely moribund.

In 1941 this situation was appreciated, at all events, by some members of the various departments of PWE. In the BBC European Service, it was certainly appreciated by the Assistant Director, Douglas Ritchie, who believed that the European Service could fulfil the role of co-ordinator of resistance. The idea was that by the daily broadcasts the BBC could act as a link between the planning authorities in England and the secret audience throughout Europe, making suggestions for action, communicating the wishes of the planners – though this could only be done in the broadest possible terms – and eventually whipping up resistance activity.

In his book *The Big Lie*[1] John Baker White has written in this connection: 'The essential of success was that the wireless campaign should co-ordinate resistance in the occupied countries. From co-ordinated resistance could spring a disciplined civilian army, acting under orders, to disrupt and slow down the working of the enemy war machine, to make life as unpleasant as possible for the occupying forces, to create fear in their minds and light the fires of hope in the hearts of the occupied.'

Experience of resistance would have shown those whose admirable objective this was, that resistance, effective resistance, cannot be organised by remote control. In saying that in attempting to organise a disciplined civilian army those behind the plan were attempting the impossible, I am not intending to detract at all from the value of the efforts made by the BBC European Service. In 1941, when the campaign originated, they were attempting to fill a vacuum, and the sense of contact, even of leadership, which was achieved was extremely valuable, for it laid the foundations of a channel of communication that in the later stages of the war was to play a major role in the activities of the Resistance. Nevertheless, it would be misleading to suggest, as Baker White does, that 'Colonels usually command battalions, but before many months had passed, "Colonel Britton" could number his soldiers, men, women and even children, in countless thousands'. The operative word here is *soldiers*, but the better word would have been *followers*, perhaps even *disciples*. The organised resistance armies – the French Maquis, the Dutch, Danish and Norwegian Underground Armies, for example – were led and controlled by men on the spot, and operated on

[1] Op. cit., p. 89.

specific orders emanating from the Allied High Command. In these armies there may have been followers of Colonel Britton, but he was in no sense their General.

Who was this Colonel Britton? Douglas Ritchie himself. The fame which he achieved throughout the world, despite what I have just said, was fully deserved.

In 1941 the Ministry of Economic Warfare was aware that the Germans were being bedevilled in their war-effort by the lack of two major commodities – copper and rubber. They were scouring every possible source of supply, and especially attics and garden sheds, refuse dumps and any other likely spot where scrap rubber and copper might be found. It occurred to Douglas Ritchie that if the occupied peoples were made aware of these German needs and could be urged to hide any copper or rubber that might be in their possession, the Nazi war-effort could continue to be hampered. In addition, by this time the Germans were beginning to conscript men and women in the occupied countries into their war-production families, and Ritchie saw that if these people could be encouraged to 'go slow', while incurring the minimum risk of punishment, this could also hamper the German war-effort.

He put forward these suggestions in a paper to the Ministry, which was impressed, and it was agreed that a co-ordinator of resistance should be created. The role fell to Ritchie.

After careful and well-thought-out preparations, one evening in May 1941 Ritchie went to the microphone and introduced himself to his vast audience as Colonel Britton. He told them what his role was and gave them his first suggestions. From then on Colonel Britton delivered his message daily.

While giving one of his talks a few weeks later, Britton referred to the V-campaign, mentioned that V in the morse code was represented by three dots and a dash, ...–, and he tapped the letter out on the table and on a glass. He pointed out that Beethoven's Fifth Symphony began with this same rhythm and that the symphony had been described as fate knocking at the door.

After a time it was decided that Colonel Britton's broadcasts ought to have a signal different from any other broadcast. The V-sign was a natural choice, and Sound Effects produced a number of variations on it. The signal eventually chosen was the V-sign played on the tympanum. Its solemn reverberating beat had an uncanny effect. According to Baker White a panzer officer told him after the war, 'We got used to the V-sign after a time. In fact, we treated it as a joke, but we never got used to the V-sound. We used to hate it. It gave me a cold feeling between the shoulder blades at night'.[1]

The V-sound was first used on 19th July 1941, and in his broadcast that followed Colonel Britton introduced a new V-campaign. 'At this moment,' he told his listeners, 'men and women all over Europe are dedicating themselves to the continuation of this war against Nazi Germany until the V – the sign of Victory and Freedom – is triumphant. In a few minutes there will be millions of new Vs on walls and doors and pavements all over Europe. It's dark now. If you listen you may hear distant bugles sounding the V-rhythm, or drums tapping. Perhaps you'll hear a train whistle sounded by one of your comrades. . . . The V-army must be a disciplined army. When the moment comes it will act in such a way that the

[1] *The Big Lie*, op. cit., p. 91.

Germans are powerless. But wait for the word. Today we sign on. Good luck to you.'

This was followed by a message from the Prime Minister, which read: 'The V-sign is the symbol of the unconquerable will of the occupied territories, and a portent of the fate awaiting the Nazi tyranny. So long as the peoples of Europe continue to refuse all collaboration with the invader it is sure that his cause will perish and that Europe will be liberated'.

The V-campaign appealed to Winston Churchill, and he had soon invented his own version of it – the right hand raised, palm facing out and the fingers spread into the shape of a V. From the impish grin that always accompanied this gesture, it seemed that the coarse signal which some gentlemen occasionally make to others when they wish to imply that they should go to hell, which needed only a slight variation in the positioning of the hand, was as much in his mind as V for Victory.

The V-campaign was most effective in those countries where there was little the people could do actively to sabotage the German war-effort, simply because there were no large, important industrial plants and railways contributing directly to the Nazi war-machine. An outstanding example of this was the Channel Islands, the only British territory to be occupied by the Germans in the Second World War, where the main industries were tomato-growing and tourism.

In his book about occupied Guernsey, *The Silent War*,[1] Frank Falla relates that 'the V-for-Victory campaign spread like a bush-fire throughout Europe and the Channel Islands and on Guernsey great white chalked Vs started to appear all over the place. . . .

[1] Leslie Frewin Ltd.: London, 1968.

"V" and "EV" were blazoned all over the Island, the most outstanding being an "EV" tarred up in the St Martin's district adjacent to the Hotel Beaulieu. I noticed nothing abnormal as I cycled home, early one morning in July 1941, but twelve hours later on my return journey as I approached the Hotel Beaulieu, I saw a large "EV" scraped in the sun-softened tar of the roadway. A few yards further on, on the biscuit-coloured entrance wall of the hotel, in tarred letters over eighteen inches high and ten inches wide, I saw another "EV". A little further along this road I saw a Nazi signpost across which was scrawled yet another "EV".'

As elsewhere, the Nazis in Guernsey took furious exception to the disfigurement of walls, roads and signposts in this way. They regarded it as sabotage, and exacted reprisals, which, in this Beaulieu case, resulted in all civilians living within a kilometre of the hotel being compelled to surrender their precious radio sets – their only contact with the outside world – and being required to mount an all-night guard over the three signposts in the area. The Bailiff (the chief Guernsey civilian authority) was compelled by the Kommandantur to sign a notice offering a reward of £25 to anyone who identified the perpetrators of V-signs. The reward was never claimed, but now and again through careless gossip people were arrested, and, as happened in the case of the one-legged, sixty-year-old Xavier de Guillebon, prison sentences were imposed. De Guillebon, who was one of the most active V-sign scrawlers in the island, went about his resistance work with an acute sense of humour. His most effective operation was the chalking of Vs on the bicycle seats of German soldiers while they were drinking in bars, so that after riding their machines their persons were embellished with Vs on the seats of their trousers.

After the Germans adopted the V-sign themselves, in an attempt to nullify the efforts of the V-campaigners, several incidents occurred the humour of which did much to keep up the spirits of the Guernseyman. A high-ranking Guernsey police officer, unaware of Goebbels's order, sent men – the Nazis required the local police to obliterate all V-signs under cover of darkness – to remove the V-signs and laurel wreathes which the Germans themselves had painted on the entrance of the Kommandantur, housed in the Grange Lodge Hotel. It took the two policemen allotted the task two hours to remove the Vs. Only when they were going off duty some time later and saw a number of V-signs and laurel wreathes on most of the important German offices, did it occur to their chiefs that the Germans might have done this themselves, a thought confirmed by the Kommandantur.

But if the German measures to put a stop to the campaign made the chalking up of signs a risky occupation, the Guernseymen, like the Luxembourgers, found ways of continuing the work to their own amusement, which was all the greater because the Germans did not understand these private jokes. Large numbers of notices appeared all over the island written thus: 'VVanted Rabbits And Fowls'. Only the initiated realised that this actually meant 'Victory – RAF'. A cinema projectionist used his spare time while German films were being screened for German audiences, to fashion English silver coins into V-brooches, with the King's head within the V. This young man, Roy Machon, was eventually caught, and sentenced to six months' imprisonment in Germany, after which he was transferred to an internment camp for the duration of the war.

The campaign, within its limitations, was an undoubted success. It led to the invention of other types of activities which probably irritated the Germans just as much. PWE suggested them to SOE who passed them on to the resistance groups with whom they were in contact.

These suggestions the Resistance eagerly put into practice, and ingenious minds everywhere thought up means of teasing the Germans to the limits of endurance.

At Niederkon, in Luxembourg, for example, all the chickens were painted red, white and blue by unknown hands, and the population stood by and mocked as German soldiers, under instructions from their officers, tried to catch the patriotic birds. The ancient fortifications of Luxembourg city contain three small towers known as the Spanish towers. The Luxembourgeois, on their journeys to work one morning, were delighted to see that during the night one of these towers had been painted white, another red, and the third blue. In vain did the Germans try to remove the paint, traces of which can be seen on the towers to this day.

In reverse, the Luxembourgeois invented similar tricks as boosters for their own morale. In a café full of Germans, one man would loudly greet another *Ola!*, and the men would laugh until the tears came at their own joke, which the Germans did not share. For *Ola* was the initials of *On les aura*, meaning in Luxembourg-French *They shall be beaten*. One father announced in the newspapers that he had shown disrespect to his forbears by christening his son Pierre; in future the boy would be called Baldur. Only the Luxembourgeois appreciated the joke; *Bal dur* in their language means *That's enough*.

At Rumelange one day, the people watched with interest a struggle between a German soldier and a factory chimney. Floating proudly 150 feet above the ground was a Luxembourg flag. The angry German sergeant rushed forward and began to climb the outside of the chimney by the iron rungs set there for the purpose, thinking to have the offending flag hauled down in no time. However, six feet from the flag he was brought to a halt – no more rungs. The unknown who had hoisted the flag had had the foresight to remove those nearest the top on his way down. It was only late in the afternoon that the flag was eventually removed by several hundred rounds of machine-gun fire.

The people of Rumelange were experts at this type of resistance. One Sunday morning, not long after the V-campaign had been launched, the *Ortsgruppenleiter* of this little town awoke to the disagreeable shock of finding the staircase leading from his apartment painted red, white and blue. The painters, however, had either been careless or their paint-pots had leaked, for trails of paint led away from the stairs. At once the *Ortsgruppenleiter* set off hot on the trail in the full expectation of catching the culprits, only to find that the paint marks led him back to his own garden overlooking a neighbouring street, where the empty tins now rested.

Perhaps the Danes invented the most effective and cruellest kind of harassment. The German troops had obeyed their orders to be friends with the Danes. The ordinary German is a sentimentalist almost without equal. He longed to be friends with ordinary Norwegians, Danes, Dutchmen, Belgians, Luxembourgers and Frenchmen. Nothing upset him more than to be treated with cold formality and correctness, from which all warmth of feeling was withdrawn – unless it was the suggestion that while he was away from home his wife or fiancée was being unfaithful to him.

The Danes, who are not without a natural appreciation of psychology, realised this. Springing spontaneously at first, but soon widely adopted by the man-in-the-street throughout the country, the policy of *Den Kolde Skulder* (the cold shoulder) became a potent weapon.

It may seem absurd, viewed in cold blood, for people to wear in their buttonholes a miniature Union Jack, or the letters DKS (*Den Kolde Skulder*) or SDU (*Smid dem ud* – throw them out), or to wear caps knitted in the colours of the RAF, or refer to the Germans always as *The Strangers*. But as morale-boosters as well as morale-destroyers they have considerable value. They raise personal morale with their sense of defiance; and when many wear such emblems they give a sense of unity.

Sooner or later such passive forms must develop into activity. The Cold Shoulder policy was soon followed by expressions of open contempt, which could be manifested in many ways. If a German military band gave a concert in a public place, it did so without a single listener but German soldiers. If Germans entered a café, at a given signal all Danes rose and left. If a German soldier presented a Wirtschafts-scheine[1] in payment, the shopkeeper would say, 'Do you mind waiting a moment, while my assistant runs

---

[1] *Wirtschaftsscheine* were vouchers given to German soldiers for use as money. The National Bank was authorised to change them into Danish money. They proved so unpopular, they were soon withdrawn.

to the National Bank to change it?' or, 'You needn't bother to give me the voucher, you may as well have the stuff for nothing.' The implications were too blatant to be missed by even the most cretinous Private.

In the cinemas, too, there was splendid opportunity. When a picture of one's beloved Führer is flashed on to the screen, it must be shattering to hear a voice inquiring loudly, 'Who is that fellow?' Or to hear a commentator announcing proudly: 'Here are one hundred of our bombers on their way to attack England,' answered from the audience by, 'Two hundred bombers returned.'

A strong sense of humour is one of the Danish national characteristics. It comes bubbling up in the most unlikely circumstances, in the most unlikely places. Thus a tram-conductor calls out, 'All saboteurs change here'; or a prisoner waiting perhaps for death, or at best the concentration camp, scratches under the two-inch-diameter spy-hole in the door of his cell: 'It is dangerous to lean out of the window'.

But it was games such as these which nurtured the spirit of resistance while it probed the raw nerves of the Germans. It is impossible to assess the value of their contribution to the psychological war-effort, but it must have been high.

Perhaps one of the most effective morale-destroyers was Sefton Delmer's campaign to sow doubts in the minds of German husbands and lovers on the sexual fidelity of their wives and sweethearts. It was a devilish campaign in its concept, but yet was certainly justified in total war. Night after night, Soldatensender Calais would remind its listeners that while they were away from home their spouses and sweethearts had no one to protect them. Not only that, separation imposes an unnatural strain on a man or woman whose sexual desires are normal. This, it pointed out, was not only true of German women but of the hundreds and thousands of foreign workers, strong, virile, finely built Norwegians and Danes, swarthy, passionate Italians, Frenchmen highly skilled in the art of seduction, that were now working in factories and fields all over Germany. Who could blame the lonely women at home if they fell to the eager, sex-starved foreigner? Indeed, should they be blamed, since by keeping the foreigners sexually happy, they helped them to enhance their war-effort.

One attempt, however, to follow up this campaign by another section of PWE did misfire. When the Germans occupied Greece and Crete, thousands of copies of a postcard in startling primitive colours, with a propaganda message on the back of it, were showered over them. The picture was of a helpless German blonde being raped by a dark Italian. But instead of it affecting the morale of the Germans, they looked upon it as an amusing 'filthy postcard', to be kept in the pocket-book and taken out on such occasions when a fantasy was required.

But if the V-campaign could not fulfil its main objective, it did achieve results that taken in sum were startling. Sugar in petrol tanks brought many a German car to a grinding halt, a write-off. Fuses mysteriously blown brought production lines to a halt, sometimes for an hour or more. Curious explosions wrecked plant in their most vulnerable spots. Fires of strange origins destroyed valuable stock.

But its greatest value lay in showing ordinary people how they could make a gesture of defiance, and thereby boost their own morale. In 1941 it was such a boost that the occupied peoples of Europe most needed.

# 8 : For Home Consumption

THE WAR OF words could be waged both ways; it could be used to lower the morale of the enemy; it was a potent weapon in raising spirits at home – provided that the speaker understood how to use words. Such a man was Quentin Reynolds.

The Battle of Britain presented the Ministry of Information with few problems. The glamour of the fighter-pilots in their Spitfires and Hurricanes coursing through the skies over the south coast was sufficient to excite and uplift the British people. What was happening over Sussex, Surrey and Kent was in the great tradition, though in a different element, of Drake and Raleigh, Frobisher and Hawkins, and later of Rodney and Nelson. This they could understand. There was no need for embellishment. Indeed it would have had to be a very brilliant propagandist indeed who could have improved upon the story that was being written above the fields, meadows and towns in September of 1940, for the straight reporting itself was the stuff of recorded history. There never was, and perhaps never will be, a script quite like it. It was David and Goliath, Horatio guarding the Tiber Bridge, the Spanish Armada rolled into one – it was that great test of the resounding days of chivalry: single combat.

The coming of the German bombers in the autumn was a different cup of tea entirely. They came under cover of darkness and their targets were those who could not hit back. As night after night the Smiths and the Joneses, the Robinsons and the Browns huddled in their cellars, their Anderson and Morrison shelters and in the subterranean labyrinth of the Underground, civilian morale could have been brought to breaking-point. It came very near, but the tenuous thread of nerve just held. And more than any other reason for its remaining intact were the broadcasts of men who were close to the people, who knew how they suffered in body and spirit, but who could give the reassurance of sanity spoken in ringing tones, because they were victims themselves but had a special talent for expression.

One voice that made people lower their evening papers or put down their drinks belonged to a roly-poly giant, a journalist, a wizard with words. What was most surprising about him perhaps, since he was intimate with the inner minds of Englishmen in agony, was that he was American.

Quentin Reynolds had been commissioned by *Colliers Magazine* to come to London to write on the Blitz from the human angle. He established himself in the Savoy Hotel and turned himself into a legend.

It began with a meeting, in a bar, with Tom Waldron, a BBC producer. Enemy aircraft were over the city, and above the noise of exploding bombs and the rattle of anti-aircraft guns, Reynolds shouted to Waldron, 'Isn't he a goddam bastard? I knew that sonofabitch in Berlin. I'd like to have a word with the bum right now!'

'So you shall,' Waldron replied, almost speaking to himself. 'So you shall.'

Four evenings later, Reynolds eased his considerable bulk into a chair in a studio in Broadcasting House, and cleared his throat. In a rich, gravelly Southern bass he addressed Hitler, person-to-person. But he did not call him Hitler; he referred to the Führer by the ridiculous name with which he had been born – Schicklgrüber.

'Sit down, Mr Schicklgrüber,' he invited the self-named Hitler. 'I want to have a little chat with you. I'm smoking a cigarette at the moment. I know you won't like that. Do you remember telling me not to smoke when I saw you in Berlin? Now I'm going to tell *you* something, Corporal. The British are going to win this war. I know. I'm watching them doing it right now. I hear, Mr S, that you are putting whistles on your bombs. Whistles! I ask you! Do you really think in your sick little mind that the British are going to be frightened by penny whistles? That, Corporal, is an insult to be avenged in blood!' After threateningly pointing out that there were 'many roads to Berlin, but you will find there is not one out', Reynolds finished by saying, almost soothingly, 'Can you imagine a man with the name of Churchill bowing the knee to a man with the name of Schicklgrüber? Really, Mr S, really!'

As he rose to leave the studio, Reynolds saw, through the glass partition, the control clapping and uproariously laughing. He had to fight his way to the lift as others patted him on the back and tried to shake his hand. When he eventually got back to the Savoy, he found a crowd of guests waiting for him in the foyer and had to engage once more in combat as he made his way to the dining-room. As he entered, every diner rose to his feet and clapped. Among the shoal of congratulations that swamped his bed the following morning was an invitation from the Prime Minister inviting him to dine that evening.

In what he described as 'a rented suit', Reynolds presented himself to Winston Churchill. The Prime Minister shook his hand for what seemed like several minutes.

'You and I, Mr Reynolds,' said Churchill, 'have much in common. We can do much together.'

Reynolds was always oddly reticent about that evening. All he would say was that his host had questioned him searchingly about Hitler, whom Churchill had never seen in the flesh. What we do know is that Churchill asked him to stay in Britain and make more broadcasts. We also know that Churchill made a tremendous impact on him, for when he was once asked what he thought of him, he replied, 'I love that man; I love him dearly.'

In his next broadcast he addressed himself to another of his Nazi acquaintances, Josef Goebbels.

'I had the misfortune,' he rumbled, 'to meet you, you palsied-minded little liar. My file on your immoralities contains over twenty sheets – all the details. Time will catch up with you, Herr Doktor. He will catch up with your lies and your tyranny. I pray I live to see the day when you lie rotting in the slime of your own making. Damn you! Damn you!'

That night the name of Quentin Reynolds was added to the Nazi list of those to be exterminated when the Germans occupied Britain.

By this time Reynolds had become one of the most famous journalists on Fleet Street. His hatred of German tyranny, and his love for those who were resolutely fighting it, were deeply sincere. He had that quality rare among American journalists that he had to feel and believe, with every fibre of his being, what he wrote; if he did not, he did not bother to write. He had a tremendous compassion for human suffering, and an abiding faith that right would ultimately prevail over wrong. On one of his two day-trips back to the United States, he told waiting reporters, 'I return with the star-dust of freedom sprinkled on my jacket.'

His books on the London Blitz, *The Wounded Don't Cry* and *Only the Stars Are Neutral*, sold in their tens of thousands, but few know that the royalties they earned were paid into a fund to help the bombed victims of Britain. This tough, hard-living bear of a man put Britain in her peril on the map; it is impossible to assess the value of what he did.

The late Paul Holt of the *Daily Express* told the story of how once, when the bombs were falling, Reynolds quietly slipped away from a party he was giving at the Savoy. When he had been gone half-an-hour Holt traced him to the hotel roof, standing against a chimney-stack with the great hotel trembling beneath his feet. He was watching his beloved London burning, his eyes wide and staring, tears coursing down his ample cheeks. He allowed himself to be led gently away. 'Put me to bed, Paul, put me to bed!' was all he could say.

Despite his genuine emotionalism he retained the tough fibre of the highly professional journalist, as Arthur Christiansen, editor of the *Daily Express*, discovered. Believing he had seen the bombing of London through, Reynolds accepted an assignment to report the war in Russia. He reported brilliantly, as always, but found that his story did not make the front pages.

'You have made me look the biggest horse's arse in the business Stop no regards Reynolds,' he cabled tersely.

There has been only one Quentin Reynolds and,

alas, he is no longer 'available for assignment.'

Reynolds could justly have claimed to be the first American in the field of psychological warfare, but his countrymen were not slow in appreciating the value of it as a weapon. Long before Pearl Harbor, Robert Sherwood, the writer of the famous plays, *The Petrified Forest, Idiot's Delight* and others, drew the attention of President Roosevelt to it one evening over dinner.

The two men had been discussing the impact of the President's *Aid to Britain* speeches, and how they had infuriated the Germans, while weaning the American isolationists from their isolationism. Sherwood, shy, six-foot, Anglophile intellectual, persuaded Roosevelt that speeches and reassurement were as vital as the arms and food he was offering, and suggested that when the time came, if it came, they should be ready and organised to exploit by every medium possible and on the widest possible front the aims of the democracies.

On leaving the White House, Sherwood was armed with what was virtually a brief from the President to explore fully what they had discussed, and so became America's first official psychological warrior. He joined forces with the British author and former agent, Robert Bruce Lockhart, Director-General of PWE, and with the US Ambassador to London, John Winant, and discussed the matter with Duff Cooper, recently appointed Minister of Information.

In the course of these many discussions he met Richard Crossman and his team of white, and Sefton Delmer and his team of black, propagandists. He assessed American needs and held 'policy talks' with Dr Hugh Dalton, Minister of Economic Warfare and responsible to Parliament for PWE. He visited the film studios and talked to writers and producers. Because of his attractive eminence he had the entrée everywhere, and by the time he returned to Washington his report was full, constructive and forceful. He battled gently but firmly with the military chiefs in the Pentagon, and he won two of them over completely – Generals Eisenhower and Mark Clark. Eisenhower, several months later, on arriving in England as Supreme Commander, informed PWE honestly, 'I'm not sure I understood all this psychological stuff, but by God we intend to make it work.'

At this stage both Churchill and Roosevelt kept themselves aloof from the new enterprise, firstly because they were deeply preoccupied in other fields, and secondly because neither of them, then or ever, fully appreciated the potential of psychological warfare. Roosevelt was of the opinion that it was a form of censorship control, while Churchill, although unconsciously Britain's 'psychological asset', refused to recognise it as a form of warfare. It is ironical that eventually it was the military who pressed the politicians for more support in this field.

The Americans had been in the 'secret' business when they were neutral. They had their embassies and observers in Vichy and French North Africa. They manned listening posts in Berlin and Rome, and sent some of their senior politicians on extensive fact-finding missions. Notable among these were Wendell Wilkie, a one-time presidential candidate, and General 'Big Bill' Donovan, later commander of the Office of Strategic Services, the American equivalent of SOE.

The role played by the journalistic world was a major one. William Shirer in Berlin was an exceptionally valuable link, while Ed Murrow in Britain was able to maintain a permanent liaison with our own organisation. Both he and Douglas Fairbanks Jr were awarded honorary KBEs subsequently for these services.

One American journalist provoked a world-wide sensation when he perpetrated a truly magnificent piece of psychological warfare. He was R H Knicker-bocker who invented a detailed story that 'proved' the Nazi leaders were salting away in South American banks vast sums of money – milched from Nazi Party funds – against the day when they lost the war. This brilliantly imaginative journalistic *tour de force* made front-page news all over the world, except in Germany and Italy, and put Knickerbocker in the front rank of international reporters. The Nazi propaganda machine, powerful though it was, was never able to counteract effectively this American invention.

Meanwhile a significant change was made at the Ministry of Information. Duff Cooper had authorised teams of fact-gatherers to call on homes, or to inter-view in the streets, a cross-section of the public. One of the national dailies, in a naughty mood, thought fit to campaign against this quite innocuous attempt to discover how people were reacting to wartime conditions. It named the people who carried out the research 'Cooper's Snoopers', and this term of abuse, more than anything else, encouraged a public outcry which became so vociferous that Duff Cooper felt compelled to offer his resignation.

Winston Churchill once more turned to a personal friend to head the official propaganda services. Brendan Bracken was fortunate in taking control of the Ministry of Information at the time that total co-operation with the Americans was almost estab-lished, for when the United States did enter the war the machinery slipped easily into motion. But it was Duff Cooper's untiring efforts that made this possible.

From the outset Eisenhower insisted that the officers of the Psychological Warfare Branch, as PWE was renamed, both British and American, should be on his personal staff, enjoying all the privileges that the personal staff of the Supreme Commander enjoyed. General Mark Clark, Commander-in-Chief of US ground forces in Europe, was equally co-operative, with the result that no planning for the Allied landings in North Africa – *Operation Torch* – was carried out without an officer of the Psychological Warfare Branch either being present or fully briefed.

Although the idea of misleading the Germans over Allied intentions in North Africa originated with PWB, the Generals authorised the necessary massive radio build-up, and the branch settled down in an advisory capacity. They were used rather as an advertising agency, called upon to develop or embellish plans already made or to suggest others. As it grew, their minds were open to anyone and everyone who had ideas that might help to confuse the enemy or raise the morale of a defeated nation.

One of the most successful leaflet campaigns ever was the brain-child of a Private soldier. But before Private Atack was inspired, PWB had to carry out one of the most macabre *ruse de guerre* in the history of deception.

# 9 : Set-piece

'BEFORE ALAMEIN WE never had a victory. After Alamein we never had a defeat.' Thus Winston Churchill closes his account of the Battle of Alamein in his history of the Second World War. It is a good *mot*, but it is not strictly accurate, for it leaves out of the reckoning the brilliant defeat of the Italians by General Wavell and his gallant Thirty Thousand in the winter of 1940 and the failure of the Allied forces at Arnhem in 1944. But in general terms it does represent the change which overtook the fortunes of the Allies from the end of 1942.

With the Germans evicted from North Africa, the Allies would have a spring-board from which to launch an attack on the Continent. They could, perhaps, have made the leap into Europe from Libya and Tunisia, but instead it had been planned to take over Algeria as well. This was an American idea, and its operation had been entrusted mainly to them. It was not expected that the pro-Nazi Vichy French, who controlled Algeria, would put up much resistance, particularly as General Giraud, who had escaped from Vichy, was to be appointed Supreme Commander in North Africa, and he was confident that he would be able to bring over to the Allies the French governors and generals, and the officer corps. But fate has a way of intervening in the best-laid plans, and decided to do so now in the shape of Admiral Darlan, Pétain's vice-premier and Minister of Marine.

In October 1942, while Montgomery was engaged in chasing Rommel out of Libya, Darlan had been on a tour of inspection in Algeria. These duties completed, he returned to Vichy. But his son, who was in Algeria, was struck down by polio and rushed to hospital very seriously ill. When the Admiral heard this news, he flew back to Algiers on 5th November.

The Allies were due to make their landing on 8th November.

The presence of the notoriously anti-British Darlan in Algeria at the moment of the Allied invasion put a very different complexion on the affair. He had considerable influence with the French governors and generals and he might be able to persuade them to put up strong resistance.

General Juin was fully aware of this new situation, and was not so egoistical as to believe that he would be able to override Darlan's influence. There was no time to work out detailed plans for immunising the Admiral, so it was decided to approach him directly and attempt to win him over.

Darlan, true to his misguided loyalties, urged the French forces to resist, but fortunately for the Allies, the heart of the troops was not in resistance, and though a show was made, it was quickly overcome. When it ceased, Darlan was a prisoner of the Americans.

It was not their intention, however, to keep him prisoner. They believed they needed the full support of the French in North Africa not only in the first phase of evicting Rommel from Tunisia, but also if the next stage of their plans was to be successfully accomplished. They believed that provided they could win Darlan over to their side, this full support would be forthcoming.

As a result of these events in Algeria, the Germans decided to occupy the whole of France, and did so with their customary lightning speed. This, in its turn, had an effect on Darlan, and when Eisenhower suggested that he should come to an agreement with the Allies, the Admiral accepted, on condition that he would be recognised as the Head of the French régime in North Africa. On 14th November, Eisenhower and Darlan signed a formal agreement to this effect.

Darlan's hatred of the British was fully reciprocated by them, and when the news of the agreement reached England it caused considerable dismay, and not only among the British but among General de Gaulle's Free French Forces. Indeed, public opinion was so roused against having anything at all to do with Darlan, and was so faithfully reflected in Parliament, that Churchill was constrained to call a Secret Session to try to damp down the fires of protest and complaint. He succeeded to a certain extent, but no one here or in France was ever happy with the arrangement.

Then fate took another turn.

The afternoon of Christmas Eve was sunny and warm in Algiers. Allied troops thronged the pavements of the rue Michèle, the terraces of cafés and restaurants were crowded. High-ranking officers gazed at the blue Mediterranean from the balconies of the Hotel Alletti, as they sipped their pink gin, momentarily content, for the fighting in Tunisia was going well.

Shortly after half past three, a Renault saloon drew to a standstill by the kerb, a hundred yards from the drive entrance to the Palais d'Eté, where Admiral Darlan had his offices. From it emerged a young man of twenty, called Bonnier de la Chapelle.

He turned into the drive and made an unhurried way up it to the unguarded main entrance of the Palais. He could hear voices coming from a room on the ground floor, and recognised one of them as Darlan's. After twenty minutes there came the sounds of footsteps crossing the marble floor of the room towards the door. The door opened and Darlan stepped into the foyer.

Calmly drawing a revolver from his pocket, Chapelle just as calmly fired five shots into the Admiral's head and chest. He then dropped the revolver and waited to be seized. Darlan was rushed to a nearby hospital, and died there on the operating table less than an hour later.

'Darlan's murder, though criminal,' Churchill drily comments, 'relieved the Allies of their embarrassment at working with him.'

Within minutes of the assassination the secret radios in Algiers were tapping out the news to receivers manned by the Psychological Warfare Branch. Eisenhower, who was having a pre-Christmas drink with his staff, at once contacted Washington and was instructed to impose a complete censorship. In London, a despatch-rider interrupted Churchill at a family gathering with a message from PWB headquarters in Norfolk House, St James's. He immediately contacted the Foreign Office and Admiral Thompson, the Chief Censor, and issued similar instructions – no Press releases and no comment for the time being.

It was only on Sunday that the Allied radio announced the bare facts of the assassination, and added that 'a youth had been arrested'. Later that day there was the further announcement that the assassin had been 'tried, sentenced to death and executed'. In less than twenty-four hours the deed had been done and the murderer disposed of. The official view was that the whole matter was now finished with and best forgotten.

But the background of the affair carries the gravest implications. In *The Hinge of Fate*, Churchill says, 'The youthful assassin had been connected with Henri d'Astier, according to some stories'.

Henri d'Astier was the brother of General François d'Astier de la Vigerie, who had been sent by de Gaulle to Algeria to find out what was going on, for the Allies, on Roosevelt's insistence, had not been informed of *Operation Torch*, the Allied landings. Henri d'Astier had led a revolt in Algiers on the day of the Allied landings and thereafter had plunged deep into a conspiracy with French monarchist elements in Algeria to bring the Pretender, the Comte de Paris, to power, and were planning to bring pressure to bear on Darlan to resign the High Commissionship, so that this could be brought about. On his return to London, a few days before Christmas, General d'Astier's report to de Gaulle decided the French leader to refuse to accept Darlan's leadership in North Africa. The question-marks raised by these facts are numerous.

During his interrogation Bonnier de la Chapelle had steadfastly refused to name any of his connections. He added, 'I am not afraid. I shall not be shot. The firing-squad have orders to use blanks.' Eisenhower, immediately after contacting Washington, had demanded that Chapelle should be handed over to the Allies. The French refused this request and, as we have seen, acted with a speed more reminiscent of the Gestapo in meting out punishment.

Of all those embarrassed by the American arrangement with Darlan, the most embarrassed were undoubtedly the Psychological Warfare Branch. *Operation Torch* had been accompanied by the largest psychological campaign so far promoted. With the entry of the Americans into the war, PWB had quickly won for itself recognition as a military arm. Units were trained at Woburn to go with the invading forces; hundreds of thousands of leaflets had been prepared for delivery to the French North African troops, explaining why the Allies were landing; radio links were established between Algeria and London.

For weeks before the landings seventeen transmitters were on the air for twenty-four hours a day. They pumped out the message, 'We are coming,' but they did not say where or when. As the giant convoys from Britain and America joined forces in the Atlantic, however, the message became more urgent. It warned the French population in northern France to move back from the coast; it hinted that the convoy might split and make a diversionary landing in North Africa, while the main attack would be aimed at France. This not only hoodwinked the French but the German High Command, too, for when the landings did take place not a single German aircraft appeared over Oran. The secret radio stations were working well a week before D-Day. Nests of loyal Frenchmen were created throughout Algeria and French Morocco. Guided, encouraged and instructed hourly they formed a fully informed clandestine intelligence service for the Allies from the moment the first landing-craft debouched its mixed cargo of troops and weapons.

Richard Crossman was in charge in North Africa and he, more than anyone else, received the full effect of the Eisenhower-Darlan agreement. Opposed to the Vichy Admiral with all the emotional fervour of which

Frenchmen are capable, the organisation of loyal men felt betrayed by Darlan's appointment as High Commissioner, and melted away.

As bad, was the awful dilemma, information-wise, in which the agreement placed Crossman. What line was he to take? What explanation could he give? What backing could he seek? It all ran counter to everything the PWB had said about the Admiral in the past. How could an object of revilement suddenly become an object of enchantment and praise? The vast following in the occupied countries and in Germany which PWB had painstakingly built up was in danger of being alienated overnight. It looked to Crossman and his staff as if all the effort, the planning and the sheer hard grind had been in vain.

Well might Crossman have echoed, though he did not, Churchill's words. The passing of the Admiral set him and PWB free once more.

On 13th May, General Alexander telegraphed to the Prime Minister, 'Sir, it is my duty to report that the Tunisian campaign is over. All enemy resistance has ceased. We are masters of the North African shore.' At once preparations began for the leap into Europe. If PWB had reached adulthood in its role in *Torch*, it was to reach a ripe maturity in its role in the landings in Sicily.

There were two alternative strategies available to the Allies in their regaining a foothold on the continental mainland; one, to land in Greece; the other, to land in Italy. Churchill had long considered Italy to be the weak link in the Axis chain – the soft underbelly of the Axis, he called it, and was to discover that the protective shell was as tough on the underbelly as it was anywhere else – and though there were those who favoured Greece, he managed to bring the majority to his way of thinking. There was already quite a definite part for the pyschological warriors to play in keeping the Germans guessing as to where the attack would come, for they were as well aware of the alternatives as the Allies.

*Operation Mincemeat*, as the ruse was called, was not the brain-child of PWB but of a Naval Intelligence officer, Lieut-Commander the Hon Ewen Montagu – now a Queen's Counsel – and some of his colleagues. It was a deception *par excellence*, however, and no account of psychological warfare would be complete without mention of it.

The planning of Commander Montagu and his team was impeccable to the last degree. They were faced with an exacting task, for somehow they had to convince the Germans that *Operation Husky*, as the next stage was to be called, was aimed at Greece, while distracting attention from the real objective, Sicily.

Montagu recalled that some time previously a member of the team had suggested dropping a corpse with a radio-transmitter attached to it into France in order to test the genuineness or spuriousness of a certain German report. The technical difficulties had made this plan a practical impossibility and it had been discarded almost as soon as it was thought of – but now, it seemed, it might be made to work.

In the Spanish seaside town of Huelva, British intelligence were aware that there was a German agent who was well in with the Spanish authorities besides being an extremely active gentleman. Montagu argued that if a dead body could be put ashore at Huelva, any documents found on him would without doubt be shown to the German agent who would pass their contents, and perhaps even copies of some of them, to Berlin.

Provided that a dead body could pathologically satisfy the Spanish medical authorities that it had been involved in an air crash at sea, the rest of the operation would be fairly easy in comparison. To make sure of this point Montagu consulted one of the greatest pathologists of all time, Sir Bernard Spilsbury, who told him that it should be possible to deceive the Spanish doctors if certain conditions were observed.

Armed with this eminent assurance, Montagu approached his superiors, who gave him their blessing, and he at once began a search for a suitable body. This proved much more difficult than one might have imagined, but eventually the corpse of a thirty-eight-year-old man was found which satisfied all Spilsbury's requirements and it was put in cold storage while the rest of what was called, with a bizarre and macabre sense of humour, *Operation Mincemeat* was completed.

Now began the task of clothing the dead body with a personality and the 'evidence'. In building up this part of the operation, it was decided that the body should be a Captain, acting Major, in the Royal Marines, an expert in certain types of landing-craft, on the staff of the Commander-in-Chief of Combined Operations, Lord Louis Mountbatten. He was being lent by Lord Mountbatten to Admiral Sir A B Cunningham, Commander-in-Chief of the Mediterranean Fleet. He was to carry with him a highly secret personal letter from General Sir Archibald Nye, Vice-Chief of the Imperial General Staff, to General Sir Harold Alexander, Commander-in-Chief of British 18th Army Group. This letter was to be the vital document, for in it Nye was to tell Alexander that the landing was to be in Greece, while it was hoped to make the Germans believe that Sicily was to be the objective.

The composition of this letter required great skill, and I quote it in full to show how very cunningly it was contrived.

Telephone: Whitehall 9400     War Office,
Whitehall,
Chief of the Imperial          London, S.W.1
General Staff.

*23rd April, 1943*

*Personal and Most Secret.*

My dear Alex,

I am taking the advantage of sending you a personal letter by hand of one of Mountbatten's officers, to give you the inside history of our recent exchange of cables about Mediterranean operations and their attendant cover plans. You may have felt our decisions were somewhat arbitrary, but I can assure you in fact that the COS Committee gave the most careful consideration both to your recommendation and to Jumbo.[1]

We have had recent information that the Boche have been reinforcing and strengthening their defences in Greece and Crete and CIGS felt that our forces for the assault were insufficient. It was agreed by the Chiefs of Staff that the 5th Division should be reinforced by one Brigade Group for the assault on the beach south of CAPE ARAXOS and that a similar reinforcement should be made for the 56th Division at KALAMATA. We are earmarking the necessary forces and shipping.

Jumbo Wilson had proposed to select SICILY as cover target for 'HUSKY'; but we have already chosen it as cover for operations 'BRIMSTONE'. The COS Committee went into the whole question exhaustively again and came to the conclusion that in view of the preparations in Algeria, the amphibious training which

[1] Jumbo was Field-Marshal Sir Henry Wilson, C-in-C Middle East.

will be taking place on the Tunisian coast and the heavy air bombardment which will be put down to neutralise the Sicilian airfields, we should stick to our plan of making it cover for 'BRIMSTONE' – indeed, we stand a very good chance of making them think we will go for Sicily – it is an obvious objective and one about which he must be nervous. On the other hand, they felt there wasn't much hope of persuading the Boche that the extensive preparations in the Eastern Mediterranean were also directed at SICILY. For this reason they have told Wilson his cover plan should be something nearer the spot, e.g. the Dodecanese. Since our relations with Turkey are now so obviously closer, the Italians must be pretty apprehensive about these islands.

I imagine you will agree with these arguments. I know you will have your hands more than full at the moment and you haven't much chance of discussing future operations with Eisenhower. But if by any chance you do want to support Wilson's proposal, I hope you will let us know soon, because we can't delay much longer.

I am very sorry we weren't able to meet your wishes about the new commander of the Guards Brigade. Your own nominee was down with a bad attack of 'flu and not likely to be really fit for another few weeks. No doubt, however, you know Forster personally; he has done extremely well in command of a brigade at home, and is, I think, the best fellow available.

You must be about as fed up as we are with the whole question of war medals and 'Purple Hearts'. We all agree with you that we don't want to offend our American friends, but there is a good deal more to it than that. If our troops who happen to be serving in one particular theatre are to get extra decorations merely because the Americans happen to be serving there too, we will be faced with a good deal of discontent among those troops fighting elsewhere perhaps

159

just as bitterly – or more so. My own feeling is that we should thank the Americans for their kind offer and we are sorry we can't accept. But it is on the agenda for the next Military Members Meeting and I hope you will have a decision very soon.

Best of luck,
Yours ever,
ARCHIE NYE

General the Hon Sir Harold R. L. G. Alexander,
GCB, CSI, DSO, MC,
Headquarters,
18th Army Group.

It will be seen that General Nye has assumed that General Alexander knew that the landings were to be in Greece, but has planted the idea in the letter by referring to reinforcements. This would, it was hoped and believed, carry more weight with the Germans, who would be justifiably suspicious if Alexander's first intimation were to be in a letter delivered to him not by a secret courier, but by an officer, albeit a very discreet one who happened to be going to his part of the world. The letter also contains another very skilful point. The code-name for the Sicily landings was *Husky*. Nye gives this name to the fictitious Greek landings; in this way, if the Germans, by some means or other, were ever to hear of *Husky* they would believe it referred to Greek landings. The code-name *Brimstone* which Nye gives to the cover-plan, that is, landings in Sicily, was entirely a fake.

To give verisimilitude to the idea that the corpse was a member of Mountbatten's Combined Operations Staff, a letter was composed purporting to originate from Lord Louis and addressed to the C-in-C Mediterranean Fleet, Admiral Cunningham, in which the alleged writer hoped Martin (the corpse) would be the man he wanted, and asking for his return as soon as possible. A second letter, from Mountbatten to General Eisenhower, was also prepared, asking the General to contribute a 'message' to be used in advertising in America a pamphlet on Combined Operations by Hilary St George Saunders, in which were enclosed two copies of the pamphlet.

The reason for these two letters in addition to General Nye's was to provide a logical explanation for the courier carrying them in a brief-case attached to his body by a chain. This mode of transport seemed essential to the planners first, because if they were carried in a pocket they might become separated from the body during its stay in the sea, and second, to prevent their becoming illegible from too close contact with water.

The body was given the name of William Martin, and the next stage of the planning consisted of providing him with a personality. To achieve this he was given an identification card, with photograph, and a number of personal letters. One of these was from the manager of his bank requiring his immediate reduction of an overdraft of £75 19s 2d, a letter to his father inviting him to lunch with his solicitor to discuss financial arrangements Martin senior wished to make for his son, a copy of a letter from the father to the solicitors setting out the terms of the settlement he required them to draft, a letter from the solicitors to Major Martin, and two love-letters from a girl called Pam, together with a snapshot of Pam. In addition there was a receipt for a diamond engagement ring, a receipt from the Naval and Military Club for a night's stay, two stubs from tickets for the Prince of Wales's Theatre, a receipt from Gieves Ltd, and a number of odds and ends – a book of stamps, a bunch of keys, a packet of cigarettes, bank-notes and coins, and so on.

Major Martin was to be conveyed by the submarine HMS *Seraph* (Lieutenant N A Jewell) to a spot off Huelva, and then put into the water. For the journey the body was placed in a special container to prevent decomposition.

The *Seraph*, with its precious cargo, sailed from Holy Loch in the early evening of 19th April 1943. On 30th April, Commander Montagu received a report from Lieutenant Jewell informing him that Major Martin had been put overboard at 0430 hours that morning in position 1480 Portil Pillar 1·3 miles approximately eight cables from the beach and started drifting inshore. Now came the waiting-time for news that Major Martin had landed.

The first intimation that all had gone well arrived on 3rd May. It was a signal from the British Naval Attaché in Madrid stating that he had been informed by the British Vice-Consul at Huelva that the body of Major Martin, Royal Marines, had been picked up by a Spanish fisherman on 30th April.

On the following day, Montagu signalled the Naval Attaché that Martin had had some very secret papers with him and he would like to know if these had been recovered with the body. The Naval Attaché, quite unsuspectingly, got in touch with the Spanish Minister of Marine, who informed him that the documents 'had been passed through "Naval channels" and would only reach Madrid via the Spanish Naval HQ at Cadiz'. The Vice-Consul at Huelva told the Attaché that he had not been able to gain possession of the brief-case or other documents but on 13th May, a fortnight after Major Martin's landing, the Spanish Chief of Naval Staff handed everything over. The brief-case was unlocked, with a key still in the lock, but the CNS assured the Attaché that 'everything was there'.

Still Montagu and his planners did not know whether their scheme had worked or not. Gradually, however, signs began to appear indicating that it might have succeeded. Inquiries at Huelva revealed that the fisherman had handed over the body to an army officer who was nearby when he landed it, and that this officer had summoned a naval judicial officer, who took charge of all the documents. It was also learned that the German agent at Huelva had heard about the body, and that he had tried to get copies of the three letters, but had failed. However, when the documents were returned to Montagu he was able to assert definitely that though the seals on them were intact, the letters had been opened, and he believed that at least one Spaniard would have seen them who would pass on their contents to the Germans.

The landings in Sicily on 10th July went well, and this seemed confirmation that the part *Mincemeat* had played had, along with other factors, been successful. It was not until the end of the war, however, that captured German documents revealed how successful it had been. Among them were copies of General Nye's letter to General Alexander, and of Lord Mount-batten's letter to Admiral Cunningham. German intelligence had behaved exactly as the planners of *Mincemeat* had hoped they would, and documents from and to German leaders showed that they had been completely deceived.

And what of Major Martin? He was buried with full

military honours in Huelva cemetery. Who he was only very few knew and they are bound not to identify him. But whoever he was, it is certain that he served his country better in his death than he might ever have done in life.

# 10 : The Inspiration of Private Atack

ON A SWELTERING AFTERNOON in August 1943, Private John Atack lay sweating, though stripped to the waist, in his tent outside the tiny village of Kouba in North Africa. High on a hill a few miles to the east of Algiers, Kouba was the HQ of GHQ 2nd Echelon – the General Office for 1st Army administration.

In civilian life, Atack was a Fleet Street journalist; in the Army he was a clerk-typist, and he did not take kindly to his duties or his rank. On this particular afternoon he was off duty and as he lay there gazing at the warships in Algiers Bay far below, his thoughts were full of the information he had picked up quite by chance that morning. The next step was Italy via Sicily, and it would be taken quite soon.

Atack knew and loved Italy and her people, whose temperament he understood. He knew they hated war, and he was convinced that with their willingness to surrender at the drop of a hat, millions of them would put up no resistance and, what was more, would aid the Allies if only they were shown what and how to do it. There and then Private Atack decided he would be their tutor.

As he walked up the hill towards the French seminary in which HQ was housed, studiously avoiding the lizards that scuttled across his path, his mind was occupied with his plan. By the time he arrived in his office and had sat down before his typewriter, he was sure that he was on to what journalists call 'a winner'.

It was mid-evening before he had completed his task and the results of his labours were on the adjutant's desk, along with his application for permission to submit it to the Psychological Warfare Branch at Allied Forces Headquarters. Two days later Richard Crossman, chief of the British section of PWB, while going through his day's mail, came upon Private Atack's letter and its enclosure. As he read it he appreciated the potential which Atack's suggestion held, and when he had finished he went at once with it to his American counter-part. The two men talked for half-an-hour, in earnest discussion of the most brilliantly simple propaganda leaflet that had yet come PWB's way.

Atack's appeal was made exclusively to the Italian civilian population. After warning them not to risk German reprisals by too obvious partisanship, he urged them to assist the Allies in every possible way. They should, he told them, keep the leaflet safely by them. They should sign the leaflet in the space provided, organise themselves into bands of one hundred, and when the Allied troops entered their town, and only then, gather in the main square. They were promised safety and an issue of whatever food supplies were available. Their leaders should collect the leaflets and hand them to the administrative officer, and place themselves at his disposal. All would then be well. White flags should be displayed to indicate that they were conforming with these instructions.

The genius of the leaflet was that it offered to a confused population riddled with fear, doubts and hunger, friendship, even unselfishness, and, above all, order out of chaos, and hope over despair. And when

Richard Crossman returned with it to his desk, it had pencilled in the top right-hand corner the word *Pantellaria*.

The almost bloodless occupation of Pantellaria, Mussolini's Malta, is not history. The former naval base actually surrendered to a Flight Sergeant of the RAF who was forced to crash-land on the island. As he flew over the fields and houses, coming ever lower in his uncontrollable machine, he was astonished to see all the roofs and windows bedecked with sheets, towels, and even white underwear. 'It looked like Wigan on wash-day,' he commented later.

When he had succeeded in bringing his aircraft to a halt and had climbed out, he found himself surrounded by Italians who kissed him, thrust bottles of wine, oranges and grapes towards him, and – hundreds of leaflets. Slightly hysterical, the Flight Sergeant radioed for instructions, and was told to stay where he was 'while we organise something'. For several hours, he held sway as unofficial Governor of Pantellaria.

The success of the leaflets on Pantellaria decided the PWB to use them elsewhere, and soon their presses were working overtime, preparing for the assault on Naples. These leaflets were printed in German and Italian, and 150,000 of them were showered over the city after the Salerno landings. There was little response from the Germans, but the Italians scrambled for the precious 'passes' to food and security; indeed, there soon developed a black-market in them.

This operation probably more than any other up to now, had the effect of convincing the Generals that they had a new and powerful weapon at their disposal. For despite Eisenhower's consistent support for

167

psychological warfare, few military commanders really understood what it was about, and looked upon the leaflet experiments as the toy of the long-haired intellectuals, who would have been better well away from all things to do with the war. Now they accepted the fact that there was something in it, after all, and Eisenhower basked in the glory of his superior perception.

The first General actually to request the services of the leaflet department was General Mark Clark, the autocratic commander of the American 5th Army. As a result, leaflet production in Tunis alone rose to seven million a week, and when the Italian campaign was well under way this figure was more than doubled, to fifteen million a week. Once established, the leaflet campaign was the means of maintaining continuous contact with the great mass of the Italian population. Taking into account the numbers of leaflets distributed and the fact that each leaflet was read by at least half-a-dozen people, it could be claimed that there were very few men, women or children in the country who did not see them. They were read eagerly, for often they were vital to the safety of the civilian. They might give forewarning of bombing attacks, thus allowing time for the Italians to put themselves out of harm's way. They were, for example, used at Monte Cassino, when all who were sheltering in the monastery were warned twenty-four hours before the attack began.

Later, leaflets were dropped warning that the railway yards in Rome would be bombed unless the Germans stopped using them. When the Germans ignored the warning, it was issued again on 18th July. When they still did not move out, on the following day the yards were bombed in broad daylight. Six minutes after the last of the raiders had withdrawn, the Allied radio stations interrupted all European broadcasts to announce the reason for the raid, and to emphasise that great care had been taken to avoid bombing the Vatican and all places of cultural and historic interest. This message was repeated hourly throughout the day. It was the epitome of the best in propaganda. It demonstrated the friendly attitude of the liberators towards the Italians and discredited the enemy's 'proof' of Allied barbarity.

By the time of the Sicily landings the strength of PWB had been significantly increased. Among the stars of the leaflet section were Richard Llewellyn, the author of *How Green Was My Valley*; Ritchie Calder, former science editor of the *News Chronicle*; Peter Noble, who was later to join the British Embassy in Rome – and Private John Atack.

In addition to these authors there was a small army of copy-writers, designers and printing experts, extracted from the armed services. The rapid growth of PWB brought with it severe problems of administration. It was, for instance, an Anglo-American operation, which meant that Allied officers and men from both countries had to live, work and eat together. To the delight of the British, the Americans were responsible for the requisitioning of quarters and the messes, and the US scales of rations were adopted, though, for reasons of discipline, the British authorities did not approve.

The question of rank also made for difficulties, for writers, journalists and artists have little regard for such niceties. Ridiculous situations therefore arose; a lance-corporal, for example, deeply engaged in mounting an operation designed to confound the enemy might find himself barred from drinking or eating with a lieutenant in charge of paper supplies.

By the very nature of their work, all PWB personnel had to be issued with permanent all-night passes and regularly found themselves being stopped in the early hours of the morning by suspicious Military Police-men. This situation was brought to a head when Lance-Corporal Lanham Titchener, who later became Deputy Director of PWB in Rome, was arrested and held in custody because he had forgotten to carry with him the necessary pass. At a stormy meeting called by Richard Crossman and his American counterpart Robert A McClure (who was Eisenhower's protégé) the authorities were compelled to accept a compro-mise. Commissioned personnel remained in their rank, while selected non-commissioned men were given civilian status. But the British military authorities remained deeply suspicious of this Fred Karno outfit, and would only allow their personnel to withdraw from their military status if placed in Class W Reserve, which meant that they could be recalled at any time and with the same rank that they had held when they had become civilians.

This almost happened to Private John Atack. While awaiting his civilian clothes, he decided to celebrate his 'freedom', in battle-dress, in the company of two American officers. Presently a junior subaltern arrived who asked Atack what he meant by drinking in a bar reserved for officers. Atack replied that the officer was actually addressing someone of higher rank than himself, and to make himself scarce.

The following morning Atack was brought up before a superior officer. 'Private Atack,' said the officer, 'your behaviour yesterday evening was disgraceful. I would remind you that the necessary confirmation that you are to be placed on the reserve has not yet come through from the War Office. Until it has arrived, you will do well to remember that you are under strict military discipline. You will be informed if – and when – you are granted civilian status. You may go.' For seven days one of the most successful of British propagandists was kept in suspense; though it is pleasant to know that he and the officer subsequently became firm friends.

The stumbling-block to normal unit control was the necessity for almost every member of the department to hold an over-all pass. Nothing and nowhere was out of bounds; travel restrictions and standing orders were rendered null and void by the production of the card which read: 'PWB PLEASE PASS IMMEDIATELY'. The holders of this card could not even be interrogated, for their work was always secret. If therefore a member was found in a dubious café in the back streets of Naples in the small hours, the Provost Marshal was powerless to inquire what he was doing there. Naturally, this led to bitter feelings among the fighting troops, and the Military Police would ignore the pass and arrest the holder on suspicion of being a deserter with forged papers.

One RASC driver, detailed to transport an Italian camera team from Rome to Paris, found himself in a nightmarish situation. In a small village, late at night, the battery of his vehicle began to fail. The camera-crew had been drinking wine from the moment they had set out, and had reached the singing stage. They were also complaining of hunger, which they ought to have appeased at PWB headquarters in Florence, and when a small trattoria came in sight, nothing would satisfy them but that the driver should stop.

Once inside the trattoria, the Italians got completely out of hand, and refused to listen to the driver's plea to go on. The beaming *padrone* was ordered to lay the table and to bring wine. Waving aside the army ration sandwiches with which they had been provided, they eventually sat down to minestrone soup, spaghetti, eggs and steak, followed by a whole cheese, washed down with numerous bottles of spumante and glasses of cognac. It was without doubt the largest black-market meal the village had ever produced.

The *padrone's* daughter had just concluded her third rendering of *Ave Maria* when the door burst open and two armed Military Policemen, followed by a number of Carabinieri, burst in. In the ensuing chaos, made worse than it might have been by the *padrone's* contin-uous shriek that he should be paid, no one seemed to be able to convey to the police that they were employed by PWB, and eventually the driver and the camera-crew were arrested. The following morning, the driver was informed that he faced charges of being absent without leave, stealing WD property, to wit, a 15 cwt truck and petrol, drunkenness and black-market activities. Further complications arose when on being consulted, PWB in Rome told the police that they had no record of him as he had been supplied to them from a vehicle 'pool' which could not be traced. However, they agreed to send someone to see him the following day.

When a young officer arrived, he was told that the driver could not be handed over to him, but that he must be returned to his own unit to face disciplinary action. The camera-crew could, however, be released if they paid 24,000 lire to the proprietor of the trattoria. As the officer had not this amount of money on him, he had to return to Rome for further instruc-tions.

On his return to the Via Veneto, he found the

relatives of the Italians installed in the hall of the film-unit building, weeping and wailing and gnashing their teeth, at which Italians superbly excel. While the military administration made desperate efforts to trace the driver's unit, the American civilian personnel officer was informed that the 24,000 lire must be deposited at police headquarters in Rome before the cameramen could be released. The legal department also became involved in an attempt to determine whether payment of the money would contravene the black-market legislation. Even if it did not, no one could decide from which account the money could be drawn or under what heading it ought to be debited.

The matter was not resolved until a conference of high-ranking Allied officers under the eagle eye of the Deputy Provost Marshal had considered the case and decided upon a compromise. But after this incident no camera-crew would agree to operate outside the boundaries of Rome except under the most urgent persuasion, nor were there any further volunteers from the driving pool.

A further illustration of the need for firm control over our new co-belligerents, with whose loyalty PWB was not so much concerned as with their enthusiasm, was provided by the Capudichino affair. It had been decided to film the rehabilitation of this small town, some twelve miles from Rome, and a British Sergeant of Italian origins, Peter Cavallero, was put in charge of a team of civilian cameramen complete with driver. As always, the curious inhabitants of the little port turned out in force to give advice and make helpful criticism.

When most of the filming had been completed, and late afternoon had arrived, it was suggested that a sequence should be taken from the opposite side of the harbour and that the tiny fishing-boats should be shot as they made for harbour with their catches. It was an excellent idea, and the Italians were instructed to proceed.

Within a quarter-of-an-hour a raft was produced and the team went aboard it, taking with them a jeep, three cameras, lighting equipment and two American still-cameramen. As the raft reached the middle of the harbour, Sergeant Cavallero decided that it would be a good time for him to refresh himself in a harbour-side café while he brought his notes up to date. He was taking his second cognac when he heard cries coming over the water. Rushing down to the water's edge, he saw that the raft was sinking rapidly, while the Italians were stripping and at the same time having a gestural altercation with the two Americans.

Within a couple of minutes or so, the raft and all its equipment sank out of sight, and the party on board struck out for the shore. Before the entire village the survivors became locked in a battle of words until all were led away to the local hotel for cognac and dry clothes.

At a subsequent inquiry no one could satisfactorily explain away the presence that day of a fully equipped diver at Capudichino.

# 11 : The Agony of Naples

As THE ARMOURED CARS, followed by infantry, cautiously nosed their way into the suburbs of Naples on an autumn afternoon in 1943, they were brought to an abrupt halt, not by German columns, but by hordes of women, fur-coated, fashionable and respectable. They were there in their thousands, begging for food. All they had to offer in return were apples, oranges, and in some cases themselves, so great was their need for something to give to their starving children. To soldiers who had up to then fought only in the desert or on the blood-stained beaches of Salerno and Anzio, this new face of war came as a deep psychological shock. The Army acted promptly and supplies were rushed up to be issued under armed guard to desperate people who fought like tigers over a morsel of bread or even a cigarette, which they could change for black-market pasta. This was a new type of war – a metropolitan war – and the need for a cease-fire was immediate, for altruistic reasons, if nothing else.

Here, indeed, was a problem of tremendous dimensions which military planning had not taken into account. We were occupying as liberators a country where all civil discipline had broken down, all communications, both road and rail, were at a standstill, and electricity, gas and water supplies non-existent. The problem was further magnified when typhoid broke out in the city for, apart from a light dusting of DDT, there was no way in which the stricken inhabitants could obtain the necessary medical supplies to prevent the epidemic from strengthening its grip. All-night queues of women holding babies, who resembled lead-faced dolls, waited outside the medical centres, which had been hastily set up, for a spray of the precious disinfectant. Malnutrition, terror and lack of sleep during the last ghastly days of the German retreat had lowered the resistance too much and the liberation of Naples in the first weeks had about it the sour smell of death and of utter despair.

The Allied High Command were quick to realise the dangers of allowing the population to suffer in this way. This was no time for sermons, no time for double-edged broadcasts. Equally, it was no time to think of convincing men and women, whose bellies were empty, of high-flown ideals of democracy and all that.

General Alexander acted swiftly. Army engineers were ordered to restore all the essential services with the help of Italian experts. The Allied Military Government were instructed to reorganise the re-quisitioning and distribution of all available food; Italian hospitals were to be given priority for medical supplies, and black-market restaurants were put out of bounds to Allied troops. These latter were a problem in their own right, for while the rest of the city almost starved to death, the *ristorante* racketeers somehow managed to serve horsemeat and chips with the occasional egg to hundreds of servicemen at fantastic prices, or, better still, cigarettes or chocolate, which were as gold in a society which lived by bartering.

The Allied Military Government performed a magnificent and speedy task in relieving a desperate situation, but it fell to the Psychological Warfare Branch, now stationed in the giant Singer sewing-machine building in the heart of the city, to act as the mouth and ears of the relief organisation. This was a new role. Within days, posters were being pasted up in the Via Roma.

The first of these posters was headed *Granai del Popolo* – granary of the people – and was composed of five photographs and short paragraphs. Picture one showed peasants harvesting wheat with a team of oxen; the second depicted two smiling women stacking wheat, saying, 'The harvest has been good, the people are filled with hope'. Number three explained that 'men and machines transform the cut-wheat into grain', while numbers four and five showed an ox-cart hauling the bags of grain, over the caption: 'Towards the granary of the people! An equitable distribution means bread for everyone'. At the bottom of the picture it was clearly stated that an Allied officer would supervise the distribution of the grain.

On the face of it, this may appear to be an extremely simple approach, but in fact it was deeply cunning, for the farmers, especially in Sicily, had been hiding their harvest fearing it might be confiscated. But reassured by this public announcement, the grain poured into the distribution centres making the promised rationing scheme possible.

Painfully, order was restored, and soon optimism began to stir once more in a people who had lived with despair for too long. As for the Allies, they had learned a valuable lesson; they were prepared for the problems that they would face in each liberated city. The country districts did not seem to present such difficulties; indeed, in some places while people in the towns were living on a bowl of soup, fifty miles away the peasants were sitting down to tables laden with veal and roast beef, a chicken or a duck.

The food crisis in Italy took high precedence with the Allied Military Government and the PWB for the remainder of the campaign. It was realised that even though the people would have to make do with the scantiest of rations, they must be told, and have it proved to them, that these would be increased only if they played their part, When grain-ships were rushed to Italy from America, newsreel teams filmed the unloading and the distribution. Volunteer corps were mobilised for fruit and vegetable gathering in the lush farmlands behind the fighting; they received full publicity. The convoys of trucks bringing the produce into the cities to the distribution centres in long unending columns put new heart into the hungry people. When supplies warranted, PWB loudspeaker vans toured all districts announcing that such and such was available. To avoid a stampede, each district was taken in turn, and it was good to see the Italian housewives excitedly making their way to the centres with their shopping bags which had lain unused for so long.

This restoration of civilian morale so early in the campaign was to pay huge dividends later in Rome, Florence and Bologna. In Naples, with the telephones restored, public transport operating again, and – perhaps most important of all – wine supplies available, the city could be seen coming to life again, the trattorias filled, and the children playing down by the harbour.

If there was any lingering regard among the population of Naples for their erstwhile German allies, it was dispelled by the attitude of the Allied troops towards the day-to-day needs of the city. Finally it was obliterated by the Germans themselves in one of their unaccountable, unintelligent and incomprehensible actions.

At one o'clock on a Saturday afternoon the whole of the city was shaken by a gigantic explosion and great clouds of black smoke billowed up into the clear sky. Shop windows were shattered for acres around the Via Roma and there was Italian panic in the streets.

The explosion had been caused by a time-bomb left by the retreating army, planted in the post office and set to go off at the busiest time of the week. Dozens of Italians were killed and hundreds were seriously maimed in this senseless affair; senseless, for the Germans knew that the building would be used only by Italians and that the act would contribute nothing to the winning of the war or delay the Allied advance in any way.

As the British, American and Italian ambulances arrived on the scene the weeping crowds lined the street and cursed the Germans. A crazed man clasped the lifeless body of his wife in his arms, shrieking '*Tedeschi! Tedeschi!*' as nearby the willing hands of Allied soldiers tore away at the rubble, searching for more victims. And as the soldiers worked, the camera-crews of PWB filmed the scene so that the world should know.

From his office across the street, the American chief of the Military Government, Colonel Poletti, commented, 'We don't have to make up anti-German propaganda – they do the job for us'.

There was a sequel to this tragedy. A high-ranking Italian officer called at British headquarters and asked for a secret interview. When this was granted he informed the officer detailed to see him that the

Germans had planted other bombs timed to explode when the electric power was switched on.

The British officer knew what the Italian did not, that the power was due to be restored that evening. Glancing at his watch he saw that it was a few minutes after four o'clock.

Dismissing the Italian he picked up the telephone to warn the engineers. There were two lines of action that could be taken, either to postpone the switching on of the current so vital to the military and civilian life of the city, while engineers searched for the bombs, or to carry on.

After fifteen minutes' consultation among themselves, Headquarters Staff briefed a PWB loud-speaker van to tour the city and suburbs ordering all civilians to remain in their homes on the ground floor until half-an-hour after the lights were restored. This order was also issued to Allied units in the city, and by seven o'clock the streets of Naples were completely deserted.

In the main power station British and American engineers waited as the minutes ticked by and 7.30 approached. American Captain Paul Elliott Smith, stationed at Vomero, high above the bay, described it as, 'eerie. We all seemed to be holding our breath as we looked over darkened Naples and wondered what would happen'. At 7.30 precisely the whole of Naples was lit up, looking momentarily like a Christmas-tree, as the street-lights flickered on for a few seconds and then were dowsed for black-out purposes. Forgotten neon lights blazed into activity, while in the houses the people blew out their candles. For half-an-hour the city scarcely breathed; but there was no explosion.

Naples presented a unique problem for the PWB. All the preconceived ideas born in Algiers and Tunis, all the abstract thinking, the brilliant radio and leaflet campaigns, disappeared under the confrontation with a starving and disease-ridden population. They had promised protection and restoration to normal life, the end of terror and privation, and freedom from 'the yoke of Fascism and the Nazis'. A cynical and hostile city waited for these promises to be implemented. There were no smiling signorinas nor garlands of flowers to greet the armies, no wine-drinking, no cheers – just desperate men and women begging for food. The soldiers became almost hardened to the sight of distracted women holding up their babies crying out *'Bambini, niente mangiare'* to the accompaniment of tears.

That the situation was brought under control within a few weeks, and order and a form of happiness and security established, was a magnificent achievement by those who seized the problem by the throat and with infinite patience and compassion transformed promises into facts. Above all, it taught the lesson that theorising is one thing, stern fact quite another. Destructive propaganda, although necessary and effective, is useless unless there can be a follow-through when the dust of battle has settled. The Psychological Warfare Branch took the lesson to heart.

# 12 : Resistance and Psychological Warfare

THE RESISTANCE IN most of the occupied countries had at least one section which fought on the psychological warfare front. As I have related earlier, the Luxembourgeois and the Danes were past-masters at attacking the morale of the Germans, the Danes with their cold-shoulder campaign and the people of the Grand Duchy with their irritating practical jokes. In Italy there was one outstanding psychological warrior – a young woman called Lily Marx.

From the moment that the North African campaign began it became increasingly obvious that the Italians had lost all heart for war, even if they had ever had any heart in it. Behind them were the defeats in Libya and Cyrenaica inflicted on them by the armies of General Wavell which had just one-third their strength. They had experienced the appalling humiliation of their campaign in Greece and they were sick and weary of the Nazi domination imposed upon them by the Germans. They shared the sombre view expressed by their Foreign Secretary, Count Ciano, who wrote in his diary as early as 1940, 'It will be a hard, hard bitter struggle from which the British will emerge victorious'.

It is certain that had it not been for the ever-watchful eye of the Nazis, Italy would have come to terms – any terms – to pull herself out of the war. In southern Italy the population were too shocked and bemused to be capable of any resistance or organised activity after the Allied landings and the strange armistice that followed with its even stranger aftermath. But in Rome there was activity.

The conditions in which Italian Resistance was born were very different from the conditions which gave the impulse to resistance elsewhere. Certainly there was confusion; but, except in the south, there was no stupor. The armistice with the Allies and the overthrow of Mussolini produced not a numbness but a totally different emotion which, at the outset, was translated into one mood, an almost general relief, and an indescribable joy that the war was over.

Had Mussolini's removal been delayed for six weeks, that is, to the moment when the Allies were prepared to launch their landing on the Italian mainland, not only might the general course of the war have been changed, but Italian Resistance might never have been evoked.

It was quite obvious that, with the Allies on the doorstep of an Italy deprived of its defence forces, the Germans would do all they could to prevent an Allied advance in the peninsula. But their efforts would undoubtedly have been weakened had those defence forces become effective after the Allies had gained a strong foothold. As it was, the period between 25th July and the Allied landings on 3rd September gave the Germans time to reorganise their own forces and bring them into Italy in considerable strength. When the Allies landed at Reggio on 3rd September, the Germans had already twenty well-equipped divisions in Italy. The twelve divisions of the Italian Army were rendered ineffective, not only by inferior equipment, but by lack of fuel which made them practically immobile. If fuel and arms could have been supplied to these Italian divisions before they disintegrated they might have been able to give a good account of themselves to the benefit of the Allies.

The premature announcement of the armistice and the flight of the King, the Government and the High Command from Rome before the Allies had consolidated their position in southern Italy, also affected the course of events. Those commanders who, like General Cadorna, held their forces intact, might have prevented a general disintegration of the army had they been supported by the authority and direction of the Government and High Command. As it was, those soldiers who had not laid down their arms and departed to their homes were seized by the Germans and, though many were able to escape, no fewer than 600,000 were interned in Germany.

It was, nevertheless, the Italian armed forces who were first in the field of resistance. As soon as the air had cleared a little, officers and men became aware of a reawakening of the old spirit of resistance to oppression, of the urge of the ideals of patriotism and liberty and of the courage of their ancient ancestors which the Fascists had been so successful in suppressing for nearly a quarter of a century.

In Rome the lead was taken by Colonel Giuseppe Montezemola. Montezemola, who had been born in 1901, was a former Chief of the Operations Bureau of the Italian High Command, and, when Badoglio formed his Government, was appointed the Marshal's secretary. He had not, however, left Rome with the Government. Earlier, in December 1942, he had been secretary at the meeting of the four Marshals – Goering, Kesselring, Rommel and Cavallero – when the enemy position in Tunisia was a matter of grave concern for them. He was, therefore, well known to the Germans and, indeed, held a number of German decorations.

Fearing a German bombardment of Rome, the High Command had designated the capital an open city, in the command of General Conticalvi. After a fortnight, however, on the pretext that the Italians held military forces there, the Germans occupied the city and arrested Conticalvi, whereupon Montezemola went into hiding.

At the end of a week he emerged and began the task of finding colleagues who had taken a similar course. Soon he was organising small groups whose primary object was to protect Rome from German destruction when the liberation of the city was seen to be imminent. It quickly became clear, however, that there were in Rome large numbers of officers and men who had gone underground, and whose circumstances, particularly with regard to their subsistence, were very straitened.

Montezemola, therefore, widened the scope of his plans. Appointed chief of the Resistance in Rome by the Government, he began to organise assistance for those underground. Obtaining money from wealthy industrialists and others, he set in motion an organisation to provide food for the large underground population, and relief for their families. As his efforts began to bear fruit, he branched out in other directions, establishing regular contact with the south and supplying intelligence to the Allies.

Resistance in other parts of Italy was also growing. In the north, those soldiers who had managed to escape arrest by the Germans had been ruthlessly pursued by the Fascist troops of the Salo Republic, and had taken to the mountains to avoid capture. There, in bands of two or three at first, and then, as the desire and will to resist grew and the introduction of forced labour by the Germans began to increase their numbers, their potentialities were recognised. Attempts were put in hand to organise and co-ordinate them.

Montezemola was of the opinion that his own efforts in Rome would be greatly assisted if a higher-ranking officer were in command of the organisation now rapidly growing. Several names were put forward and eventually General Armellini was appointed.

Under the Fascist régime there had been a certain clandestine organisation set up under the auspices of the Communists. Since the overthrow of Mussolini these small groups, believing that their hour was at hand, had become more active, and though at first disappointed by the turn of events, they anticipated the eventual outcome and continued their work underground. Montezemola's second aim was to co-ordinate all activities of a clandestine nature. A Committee of Liberation, composed of the six political chiefs and Montezemola as the military representative, was set up, and the Colonel believed that his hopes for co-ordination were about to be achieved when tragedy overtook him.

In his zeal Montezemola had taken risks which normally should not be taken by so important a figure in underground activity. Though ably assisted by Colonel Giovanni Pacinotti, whom he had appointed as his Chief of Staff, and other highly competent officers, he kept the reins of his organisation completely in his own hands. Besides this, his personality was such that no one was able to resist his appeals. He knew it, and such was the problem confronting him of the great and ever-increasing number of men now underground in Rome who had to be supported and fed, that he moved about among various circles of his supporters too freely for security.

On 25th January 1944, as a meeting of the leaders was dispersing, the Gestapo pounced. Montezemola had stayed behind to discuss a particular problem with one of his staff, and as General Armellini and his secretary, the Marchese Multedo, left the house they were aware of men watching the entrance. It was impossible for them to go back to warn Montezemola without endangering themselves. It later became clear that the Gestapo were anxious to capture Montezemola at all costs, and that they had identified their quarry.

As Montezemola came into the street he was seized at once. He was taken to the notorious Via Tasso where was situated the most infamous torture chamber in all occupied Europe. But although the Germans applied every means, they could not make their prisoner talk, and he was able to warn in time most of those associates whose names he had carried about with him in a pocket-book.

As a result of Montezemola's keeping the details of his organisation to himself, General Armellini, who had only been appointed Commander of the Resistance in Rome a very short time before, was placed in a very difficult position. He had not yet become fully conversant with all the ramifications of the organisation, and with Montezemola *hors de combat* he was ignorant of many of the Colonel's lines of contact.

General Armellini was a regular soldier, and had all the regular soldier's distrust of politics. This made him unsympathetic to the politicians and created difficulties which, it later became apparent, could not be resolved while he remained in command. As it was essential that there should be complete solidarity of views between the military and political components of resistance, Armellini was eventually replaced.

The Communists had always been actively anti-Fascist. They were, at this time, certainly the best organised of all the political parties underground, and they were not content merely to organise in order to protect Rome from destruction when the time came, but were intent on harrying the Germans at once. They organised small groups of three or four men, known as GAPs, Patriotic Action Groups, whose role was to carry out sabotage and small-scale attacks. Later, GAPs were organised by the other political parties, but for the time being they were a purely Communist manifestation.

There is in Rome, in the hinterland of the Via Tritone, a small street called the Via Rasella. In the Via Rasella on 23rd March 1944 the Communists placed in a hand-cart a bomb which exploded as a squad of SS were marching by. Thirty-two Germans were killed.

With surprising speed the enraged enemy cordoned off the area and from the people found in it they selected hostages. The following day these hostages, to whom were added men who were already in prison to bring the total up to 335, were loaded into lorries and driven out of Rome to the Ardeatine Caves. There all 335 were shot, and among the sixty officers who were included in the hostages was Colonel Monte-zemola.

As 1944 progressed, the work of organisation continued, and help began to come in from the outside. Up in the northern mountains the SOE and OSS made contact with the various groups, whom they trained and armed. There and in the south the PWB also played a significant part. It produced a news-sheet which was circulated by certain groups to the ordinary population, giving the man-in-the-street a truer picture of what was happening than he could get from other sources, boosting morale and encouraging underground activity. In their contacts with the underground, PWB were the recipients of much useful intelligence, which not only helped them with their own special activities, but was often of the greatest use to the military authorities.

Among the groups which co-operated with PWB in this way was that to which Lily Marx belonged. Strikingly beautiful, she could have been a highly successful model; in fact, she was one of the most ruthless resistance workers PWB knew. Without firing a shot or causing a single explosion, she and her friends bedevilled the Germans, for they provided services without which no clandestine organisation in wartime can successfully exist – forged identity papers and ration cards, and lines of communication between liberated and occupied Italy. There was not a forger or a printer in Rome whom Lily did not know and could not 'persuade' to help her. At a moment's notice, a member of the underground could be supplied with a travel-pass and a railway ticket. She knew the photographers and retouchers who could produce little miracles in changing a picture to make it resemble the bearer, and she intuitively knew the reliable from the unreliable.

She had a curious history which made her particularly suited for this work. She was half-German and half-Russian, and she could read, write and speak fluently in five languages. She had a deep hatred of the Germans which sprang from the fact that she was partly Jewish and a direct descendant of Karl Marx. In the event of a Nazi victory, she realised that culture would be the first casualty, and that her beloved adopted Italy would be a major victim.

There were strict rules for these PWB associates to observe. Each had a code-name, and when they made contact it was always from a public telephone box, the same booth never being used twice. Every restaurant, café and bar in Rome, at some time or another, was used for passing on information or putting into circulation the timing of a PWB broadcast, and so on. They met in attics in the Pantheon district; they exchanged information in the Turkish baths; they strolled as lovers in the Borghese Gardens; the public lavatories vied with the post-offices for the passing of messages.

All the time the shadow of the Via Tasso was there, and, despite their vigilance, too many disappeared behind those sinister doors. Each one had much to tell, but only a small handful of them cracked under the ghastly tortures. Those who believe that the Italians lacked courage would do well to learn of their resistance.

Lily Marx created a skilful cover for her activities. She cultivated the café society clique, with its blend of ancient Roman aristocracy. She was a frequent guest of the Borghese family. Every hotel bar and smart restaurant knew her and she had many admirers and escorts. Those who could be useful to her, she played up to, and a good deal of information came her way at the candle-lit tables of Alfredo's or Giuseppe's and eventually reached PWB monitors in Naples within minutes of her closing the door on her unsuspecting escort. She worked by day and met her contacts openly. A laughingly scribbled note passed over the table would tell of the escape of Allied prisoners of war making their way to the Abruzzi mountains down the escape-route from the north.

This road to safety, known as *Operation Peak*, consisted of elaborate chains of communication between the mountain villages. The people of the mountains were shown special honours when the Allies captured Rome, and Alexander Mackendrick's film unit made *Abruzzi Devastate* to raise funds for those who had risked their lives for the Allies and were now starving and in rags.

There were many like Lily in the cities of Italy, but she is the outstanding example of those who used their intelligence, talents and courage to confound the enemy with every means and artifice that could be devised.

Opposite the Excelsior Hotel on the Via Veneto in Rome is an elegant flower-shop. Crystal-clear water cascades down the wall of glass and green-overalled Italian girls arrange and rearrange the masses of roses, carnations and orchids which give it a rare scent.

Behind the shop itself, down three curving steps, is an intimate cocktail-bar frequented by lovers and by those who need seclusion in which to discuss their affairs. On a September afternoon in 1943 Lily Marx smiled at the assistants as she made her way to this bar where she was greeted by Ettore Basevi. He kissed her hand, and she asked for a large glass of hock. In this way Basevi learned that the feared German occupation of the city had begun.

A little later she and Basevi joined the crowds at the Colosseum watching the columns rattle past. She noticed that there was an absence of heavy equipment; no artillery, no mortar units. There were anti-aircraft guns, and the soldiers jammed into the transports were conventionally armed, but the clear picture that emerged was that the Germans had no intention of turning Rome into a battlefield. The occupation of the city could, therefore, be only for prestige and, of course, as a security measure.

Right up to the day the Allies liberated Rome detailed daily reports reached Naples on every aspect of the occupation of the city. PWB knew what scale of rations was being issued to the troops; it knew the attitude of the Italian girls to the German soldiers; the behaviour of the soldiers towards the civilians; and, in the case of the Ardeatine Caves Massacre, the names of the members of the firing-squads and their officers and NCOs. They also knew the state of the city's fuel and water supply and, above all, had right up-to-date reports on the civilian food situation. With the experience of Naples always in mind, these reports were of first priority value.

One evening while dining with friends in a villa belonging to an Italian officer deserter and his English wife, Lilian Harvey, Lily received some disturbing news. The telephone had rung, and when Lilian's husband returned from answering it, he told them that the Germans were making inquiries about the activities of Lily and Basevi.

Later Lily said that as they sat by candle-light looking through the windows at the city below them, for a moment it seemed that the room was penetrated by an icy coldness. 'I was paralysed with fear and for a time could not think or move. All I knew was that I had to go and find Ettore, provided he was not already arrested and in the Via Tasso.'

Lilian's husband got her coat and hurried her to the centre of the city in his motor-car. As he got in beside her she saw that he had put a revolver in his coat pocket. Without lights they set off down the hill, and as they went he kept pressing her hand and assuring her over and over again, 'You'll be all right'. When they reached the almost deserted Via Nazionale, Lily stopped him, saying it would be safer to continue on foot. They kissed lightly and he drove away. She did not know that they would never see one another again.

Fearfully she turned into the avenue where Ettore lived with his parents and, with a last look over her shoulder, she unlatched the great gates and ran up the long path to the front door. She rang and the door opened, and there he was, safe with a wine-glass in his hand.

When she told him what she had heard, he poured her some wine and sat down. He was completely calm and confident. 'Tomorrow,' he said, 'we will go to my friend in the Vatican and we will be married and then they will give us sanctuary until the Allies arrive.'

And that was what they did. At eleven o'clock the following morning they were married and refuge was granted them. When the Allies liberated Rome, they were in the streets greeting the armies they had helped so much. Later both were given important posts with the PWB, Ettore on a newspaper and Lily as co-editor of the illustrated magazine *Il Mondo Libero*.

When the husband of Lilian Harvey dropped Lily at the Via Nazionale, he drove to the other side of Rome to warn another couple that the Germans were looking for them. On the way a patrol stopped him; he pulled his gun and was shot dead.

# 13 : What Justification?

In *The Big Lie*, John Baker White recounts an incident in which he was involved after the war. He found himself one day in the company of a high-ranking officer who had heard that White had been employed on special work and asked him what exactly he had done. When White explained briefly, the officer scowled, exclaimed that he was ashamed that his country had sunk to such depths in waging war, and turned on his heel.

It is difficult to understand the mentality of such an attitude; and the only consolation is that the generation to which the General belonged was fortunately fast dying out, its opinions rapidly losing any influence. The days when war could be waged with 'honour and chivalry' have passed. Nowadays, even in the localised conflict of the type of Vietnam, or the internecine civil war of Biafra, it is no longer possible for the struggle to be waged by military forces alone; the civilian population are engaged on such a scale that what used to be called the Home Front is now as much part of the Front Line as the confronting forces on the battlefield. The Second World War, which introduced the concept of total war into military history, destroyed for ever the possibility of separating civilians from the military in any conflict henceforth. Armies are organised on such a vast scale that they can be kept in the field only by the efforts of the great mass of the civilian population behind them. This being so, it can surely be argued with justification that since armies cannot remain in the field without the support of the civilian population, it would be militarily stupid to ignore the latter as a target of first-class importance. Put simply: the sooner the factory-workers, the train-drivers, the food manufacturers are made *hors de combat*, the sooner must their professional military counterparts be rendered ineffective, and therefore defeated. That total war is to be the war of the future – as it was in the Second World War – has been underscored by the nuclear strategy which has been adopted by all armies likely to be involved in a major conflict.

If, then, entire nations are to be directly involved in war, and the object is to secure victory by the quickest knock-out of the sources of supply for the armies, not only bombs and shells may justifiably be rained upon civilians and soldiers alike. Every weapon that is in the armoury can be brought to bear; in fact, *should* be brought to bear; for the sooner the enemy is crushed, the less protracted will be the sufferings of all concerned. Modern warfare, with its nuclear and bacteriological weapons, is such a hideously uncivilised business that attempts to weaken the spirit of the enemy by psychological means must *ipso facto* be justifiable.

The word *psychological* – all too readily confused these days with *psychiatry* – has achieved in many minds a sinister connotation which it does not possess, and it is this sinister connotation which, I believe, produces a revulsion from any suggestion that it should be used as the basis for a weapon of war. It is remarkable, in my experience, how many people can accept the use of nuclear weapons with only an initial revulsion – and even this may be short-lived –

but who will rant long and loudly against the process known as brainwashing. Yet brainwashing is really what all psychological warfare is about, for it is but an extreme form of this kind of warfare. Accepted that the use of psychological weapons is as legitimate as the use of the nuclear bomb in the conduct of *total* war, brainwashing, which aims at neutralising potential opposition, is equally justifiable. Anything which will shorten the ghastly war of total weapons must be acceptable, for there is nothing to indicate that the brainwashed subject is any less capable of happiness after the process has been effectively applied to him, than he was before.

Compared with the operation of brainwashing as we now define it, what the psychological warfare warriors were trying to do to the German soldier and civilian was a mild operation. In brainwashing the initiative is taken from the victim; but had the Germans taken stock of the propaganda to which they were being subjected and had brought an objective attitude to bear on their situation, they could have retained the initiative by telling themselves that this was enemy propaganda. That they succumbed to it cannot be laid at the door of the black propagandists; they can blame only themselves that they allowed their morale to be undermined by the lies. Nor is it any advantage to them to claim that they had already had their judgment weakened by events. The man of spirit and courage can rise above whatever onslaught to which he may be psychologically subjected, whereas unless he has a shelter and protective clothing he cannot escape the consequences of a nuclear explosion, even as he is equally vulnerable to the effects of traditional weapons within whose range he happens to be.

It has been customary to judge the success of a weapon by the extent of the havoc it causes. The PWB attempted to justify their activities by the extent to which their particular kind of warfare influenced the outcome of the war. Sefton Delmer, in *Black Boomerang*, has admitted that after the war he tried to obtain an assessment of the success this or that campaign had had.

It is futile, if human, to try to gauge the measure of success. The only justification for wanting to know how successful the PWB effort was, is to be able to judge its total effectiveness, since it was not possible to make an assessment after each campaign. But this is a pre-eminent case in which the justification is not to be assessed by the end-result. In total war, though the greater the success the sooner the conflict will be resolved, every little counts, probably as in no other sphere of human activity. If the morale of only two or three were weakened by the black propagandists' efforts, those efforts, though vastly in excess of the energy expended, were worthwhile and justified. It was an addition to the total war-effort which might vitally affect the ultimate outcome.

As for the ethical considerations, these do not exist; the concept of total war is accepted as the basis for waging war. Personally, I am quite unable to understand the attitude of those who oppose black propaganda on ethical grounds. I have met no one in this category who has opposed the practice of espionage as a *sine qua non* of national existence. Yet the success of the spy is based entirely on his rejection of all normal moral codes. As soon as a man adopts the role of spy, he takes upon himself the role of deceiver, and if he develops into a successful spy the role of deceiver *par excellence*. Lies and deceptions, and betrayals of confidence and trust – these are the essential ingredients of espionage, just as they are the essential ingredients of psychological warfare, but with this difference – they must be more total, reject ethical considerations more wholeheartedly than psychological warfare requires of them.

As it turned out, it was possible to reach some assessment of PWB's campaigns by diligent inquiry after the war and to be able to claim justifiably, on this basis, that all PWB's efforts had borne a not inconsiderable fruit. So long as the psychological warriors were able to remain uncorrupted by their work – and there is not a single indication that even one of them was unable to rehabilitate himself ethically when his work was finished – no harm was done; on the contrary, only good, from their and our points of view, accrued.

# Index

*Achilles*, 105, 106

*Ajax*, 104, 106–7, 108

Alexander, General Sir Harold, 155, 157, 160, 163, 176

*Ark Royal*, 107

Armellini, General, 187, 188–9

Astier, Henri d', 153

Atack, Private John, 147, 165–6, 169, 170–1

*Athenia*, 40

Atlantiksender, 69–72

Baker White, John, 51–2, 128, 130, 195

Baldwin, Stanley, 25, 36, 91–2

Banks, Brigadier Sir Donald, 95, 97, 98

Basevi, Ettore, 192, 193, 194

Beaverbrook, Lord, 45, 55

Bethmann-Hollweg, Theobald von, 11

Bracken, Brendan, 94–5, 146

Bradley, General Omar, 88

Braun, Max, 64, 66

Brooks, Major-General Dallas, 73

Cadorna, General, 185

Calder, Ritchie, 169

Cavallero, Peter, 173–4

Chamberlain, Neville, 25, 29–30, 32–4, 36, 37, 39, 40, 41, 45, 46–7

Chapelle, Bonnier de la, 152–3

Child, Clifton, 69

Christiansen, Arthur, 143

Churchill, Winston, 39, 40, 42, 45, 47–8, 50, 57, 60, 62, 63, 92, 94–5, 97, 98, 104, 131, 141–2, 145, 146, 149, 151, 152, 153, 155

Ciano, Count, 183

Clark, General Mark, 145, 147, 168

*Clement*, 104, 105

'Colonel Britton', 128–30

Connor, William, 45–6

Conticalvi, General, 186

Cooper, Duff, 48–9, 56, 58, 144, 146

Crewe House, 14, 15, 16

Cripps, Sir Stafford, 63

Crossman, Richard, 58, 64, 144, 154–5, 166, 167, 170

Cudlipp, Hugh, 45–6

*Cumberland,* 105
Cunningham, Admiral Sir
  A B, 157, 161, 163

Dalton, Dr Hugh, 41, 144
Darlan, Admiral, 150–2, 153,
  154–5
De Gaulle, General, 151, 153
Delmer, Sefton, 55–61, 63–5,
  67–70, 72–3, 75, 76–84, 85,
  86–9, 137, 144, 198
Der Chef, 60–8, 84–5, 87
Donovan, Colonel 'Big Bill',
  76, 145

Eastwood, Sir Ralph, 109,
  110, 118–20
Eberstein, Freiherr von, 73
Eisenhower, General,
  145, 147, 151, 152, 153,
  154, 159, 161, 167–8, 170
Ernst, Albrecht, 64
*Exeter,* 105, 106, 107

Fairbanks, Jr, Douglas, 145
Falla, Frank, 131
Fleming, Ian, 67
Foley, Major, 109, 118
Fritzsche, Hans, 64

Girand, General, 149
Godfrey, Admiral, 67–8
Goebbels, Josef, 17–23, 29,
  30, 38–9, 40, 41, 43, 56,
  65, 70, 71, 73, 83, 91, 92,
  133, 142
Goering, Hermann, 36, 38,
  39, 92, 94, 125, 185

*Graf Spee,* 104–8
Graven, Dr F H, 95
Guillebon, Xavier de, 132
*Gustav Siegfried Eins,* 60–1,
  63–4, 67–8, 84

Hannibal, 101, 103
Hardiman, Captain Eric,
  95–6, 98
Harvey, Lilian, 193, 194
Harwood, Commodore Henry,
  104–7
Hervey, Lieutenant Jack, 113
Hess, Rudolf, 60, 61
Heywood, Brigadier, 116,
  120–1, 122
Himmler, Heinrich, 85, 86–7
Hitler, Adolf, 11–12, 16–17,
  18, 19, 20, 29, 33–6, 43,
  44, 49, 56–7, 59, 64–5, 83,
  84, 86, 88, 89, 92, 94, 100,
  123, 142
Holt, Paul, 143

Ingrams, Leonard, 58, 59, 63

James, Lieutenant M E
  Clifton, 110–23
Jewell, Lieutenant N A, 162
John, Otto, 85
Juin, General, 150

Kennedy, Hon Joseph, 31–2
Kirkpatrick, Sir Ivone, 72–3
Knickerbocker, R H, 146

Laelius, 102
Langbehn, Dr, 85–6
Langsdorff, Captain, 105–8

Laveleye, Victor de, 125, 126
Lester, Colonel, 111–12, 113, 115, 118
Ley, Dr Robert, 84–5
Liddell, Alvar, 38, 40
Llewellyn, Richard, 169
Lockhart, Robert Bruce, 73, 144

Maass, Alexander, 64
Machon, Roy, 133–4
McClure, Robert A, 170
McCurdy, Dr J T, 77
McLachlan, Donald, 88
'Martin, Major William', 161–4
Marx, Lily, 183, 190–4
Monroe, Captain James, 79–80
Montagu, Lieutenant-Commander the Hon Ewen, 156–7, 162–3
Montezemola, Colonel Giuseppe, 185–9
Montgomery, General, 108–18, 120, 150
Mountbatten, Lord Louis, 157, 158, 160, 161, 163
Murrow, Ed, 145
Mussolini, 30, 74, 167, 184, 187

Niven, Colonel David, 111
Noble, Peter, 169
Northcliffe, Lord, 12–17, 19, 27, 33
Nye, Sir Archibald, 157, 160, 161, 163

Obermeyer, Sepp, 78
*Operation Husky*, 156, 158, 160
*Operation Mincemeat*, 156–7, 163
*Operation Torch*, 147, 153, 154, 155
Owen, Frank, 49

Pacinotti, Colonel Giovanni, 187
*PLUTO*, 99
Poletti, Colonel, 179
Popitz, Johannes, 85
Priestley, J B, 49, 64

Reinholz, Johannes, 64
*Renown*, 107
Reynolds, Quentin, 64, 139, 140–4
Ribbentrop, Joachim, 35, 36
Ritchie, Douglas, 125, 127, 129
Robson, Karl, 69
Rommel, 108, 123, 150, 185
Roosevelt, President, 29, 41, 76, 144, 145, 153
Rosenberg, Alfred, 18

Sanders, Corporal Paul, 63
Scipio Africanus, 101–3,
*Seraph*, 162
Sherwood, Robert, 144
Shirer, William, 49, 57, 145
Sibert, General Edwin L, 87–8
Smith, Paul Elliott, 180
Soldatensender Calais, 72–5, 78, 80, 83, 84, 86, 137

Spilsbury, Sir Bernard, 157
Stalin, 29, 35
Stanley, Oliver, 25, 43
Stauffenberg, Count, 84
Stern-Rubarth, Dr Edgar,
    15–16
Stevens, C E, 69, 72
Stokes, Richard, 57
Strasser, Gregor, 19
Stuart, Sir Campbell, 14–15,
    33, 36–7, 39, 41, 48
Syphax, 101–3

Thimme, Hans, 14

Titchener, Lance Corporal
    Lanham, 170

Versailles Treaty, 11, 12, 134

Waldron, Tom, 140
Watts, Captain Stephen, 113
Wavell, General, 149, 183
Wilkie, Wendell, 145
Wilson, Field Marshal Sir
    Henry, 158, 159
Wilson, General, 121, 122
Winant, John, 144
Wood, Sir Kingsley, 32